RISE UP AND BUILD

RISE UP AND BUILD

Nick Cuthbert

KINGSWAY PUBLICATIONS
EASTBOURNE

Unless otherwise indicated, biblical quotations
are from the Revised Standard Version
copyrighted 1946, 1952, © 1971, 1973 by the Division
of Christian Education of the National Council
of the Churches of Christ in the USA.

Quotations marked with an asterisk are
the author's own rendering.

NIV = New International Version
© New York International Bible Society 1978

AV = Authorized Version
crown copyright

Printed in Great Britain for
KINGSWAY PUBLICATIONS LTD
Lottbridge Drove, Eastbourne, E. Sussex BN23 6NT by
Richard Clay (The Chaucer Press) Ltd, Bungay, Suffolk.
Typesetting by Nuprint Services Ltd, Harpenden, Herts.

Contents

	Foreword by David Pawson	7
1.	Another book?	11
2.	Forget the former things	18
3.	Jesus weeps for his church	28
4.	Power, pride and pleasure	46
5.	What are you building?	55
6.	The body of Christ	62
7.	New structures for old	71
8.	Rise up and build	78
9.	Power from above	87
10.	Into battle	92
11.	Evangelism and the body	105
12.	I have a dream	117

Then I said to them, 'You see the trouble we are in, how Jerusalem lies in ruins with its gates burned. Come, let us build the wall of Jerusalem, that we may no longer suffer disgrace.' And I told them of the hand of my God which had been upon me for good, and also of the words which the king had spoken to me. And they said, 'Let us rise up and build.' So they strengthened their hands for the good work.

Nehemiah 2:17–18

The harvest is plentiful, but the labourers are few; pray therefore the Lord of the harvest to thrust out labourers into his harvest field.

Luke 10:2*

The tide has turned

by

DAVID PAWSON

Renewal, restoration and revival. The three R's of contemporary Christian debate. Some think they are mutually exclusive concepts. Others see them as consecutive phases. A few, including the author, realize they belong together. Reality usually has three dimensions.

Renewal is essentially personal and brings us into a dimension of blessing. Restoration is essentially communal and brings us into the dimension of building. Revival is essentially national and brings us into the dimension of battling.

This book everywhere assumes renewal and anticipates revival. But Nick's main burden is for restoration. He shares this with many other men around the country (while the Lord appears to be laying the burden for revival primarily on the women, as they intercede for the nation).

Don't be put off by the mixed metaphors (waves, walls, winds, wineskins, wives!). There is good scriptural precedent in the prophets and the parables of Jesus. Paul originated the one which you will meet most frequently—*building the body*.

We see the church through the eyes of a radical, in the true sense of that word. Not someone who goes way out, but someone who gets right down. Digging out the *roots* of the problem in order to lay good foundations.

It is easy to diagnose the main troubles as professional-type ministry and club-type membership. To probe beneath these to the pride and fear which underlie them is a bold step. How to lose friends and influence people! Prophets were never popular.

7

They have to pluck up as well as to plant, to destroy as well as to build. Yet the ultimate thrust will be positive. It is here.

We are called to build a network of relationships in every locality. This is, I believe, top priority for the eighties. Without such a net we will not be ready for the great catch of fish. Many are swimming towards us but they could swim right past us.

Most will be familiar with the threefold tier of fellowship—cell, congregation and celebration. The first and third are now well established, though not yet in sufficient quantity or quality. It is the middle one that requires most urgent attention. Cells are too small for body life, celebrations are too big. But most of what we *call* 'congregations' are anything but! Usually led by one man exercising his gifts of 'conducting' many anonymous worshippers (invariably in rows), they hardly resemble New Testament come-togethers (the meaning of both 'synagogue' and 'congregate'). Mutual ministry under corporate leadership is missing.

Here comes the crunch. We can *add* cells and celebrations to our existing structures (with a certain strain on the diary!). But to build congregations we must *alter* existing structures. New wine won't go into old wineskins—the fermentation causes a rigid vessel to burst. Is the only way to go for totally new structures? Should we all leave the old denominations and join the 'house churches' (most of which don't meet in houses!)? There is another possibility—put a new wineskin inside the old one! The old one will still burst, but no wine will be lost.

This would call for courageous leadership. Men who will not lose their identity or security when the old one goes. Men who will face the religious establishment in the same spirit as the Lord and his apostles faced theirs: 'We must obey God rather than men.' We will need teachers who will listen to the prophets, pastors who will recognize the apostles. The local leaders will need to regard the total body of Christ in the area as their *first* priority and loyalty—and commit themselves to each other in costly friendship.

Only men willing to die need apply. Men who will let go their reputation, their success, their position, their monopoly, their pension. Men who have seen how silly it is to build sand-castles when the tide is coming in.

For the tide has turned. It is still a long way down the beach and is flowing slowly in at first. Yet the political, commercial and entertainment worlds all show an awareness of a religious revival. To quote the editorial of a political publication: 'A renewed demand for access to non-material values is generating the supply to meet the demand. This could be the start of something quite spectacular.'

But will the church be ready? Many would be glad to 'get converts' but few are ready to 'make disciples'. To use another mixed metaphor, good fishing demands good shepherding. Could the many disappointments we have had after big crusades ('Well, it did us good, anyway') be explained by the fact that God only gives us as many spiritual babies as he knows we can handle? On the day of Pentecost each believer had twenty-five new brothers to care for!

But the early church also had opposition. The first wave came from within 'sacred' circles and the second from 'secular' society. The first prepared them for the second. If we can't handle opposition from within our own religion we are not likely to stand when it comes from other religions and none. Yet behind all human hostility lies supernatural hatred. This book rightly analyses the nature of the struggle and the decisive factors in it. It is good to see young Nick tackling old Nick so effectively!

One final and personal word. Those who have listened to us both will wonder how much collaboration there has been between us! Does *he* write what I say or do *I* say what he writes? There is certainly an astonishing similarity between us. The answer is that until he asked for comments on his completed manuscript I had little personal knowledge of his thoughts. Our paths had been separate but parallel. I was thrilled to have the encouragement of finding a like mind. The truth is we both got it from the same source. We both believe we have received our burden from the living Lord. We do not believe we have the right answers but we do believe we are asking the right questions. We also both want the Lord to get every bit of the glory. Without him there would be nothing to say and without him there would be no results from saying it. Don't read it without him either!

J. David Pawson

1

Another book?

'Not another book on the church!' commented a friend when he heard of my intentions to sit down and write. 'Not another book!' cried another. 'There are already far too many Christian books on the market. And most of these are being read by such a small number of people.'

I knew they were right. Books today are rather like so many sermons; listened to, enjoyed, shared and then forgotten in the mad rush to move on to the next. If we as the church in Britain fail, it will not be because we have not *heard* either by the spoken or the written word, but it will be because we have failed to take seriously what we did hear. Hearing is only real hearing when it results in doing.

There was a vicar once who preached the same sermon for five consecutive weeks. After the fifth time of repeating the sermon, certain members of his congregation complained that he ought to be producing new material. He replied, 'But you haven't heard this one yet.' When they questioned him further, he explained that until they began to apply what he said he presumed they hadn't yet heard it! If there are too many books being produced about the church, it may be because we haven't yet heard what they are really saying.

We in the church in Britain need to be very careful that we don't become like the man who built his house upon the sand. He heard all right, but he failed to obey. The tremendous interest in church growth seminars is certainly one indication that many people are looking for a change in their church situation. Whether

11

they apply what they hear is another thing. For there will be a cost if it is to be anything more than a superficial change.

Have you read?

How many have read *Rich Christians in an Age of Hunger*? It certainly made many of us feel very guilty—but what did we actually do in response to what we read? How many have read *Celebration of Discipline*? No doubt it deeply challenged many of us concerning our own personal Christian lives, but what have we done to express what we heard? I wonder who has read Howard Snyder's superb book *New Wineskins* and felt that what he was saying was absolutely true of the church today. But what did we actually do in response to it? Again and again many of us are guilty of reading things or hearing things, to be deeply challenged by them but then only to put them aside again. I am not saying this to twist your arm into doing what this book suggests! I am making a plea for all of us to examine whether or not we are being obedient to what God is saying to us today, however painful that might be.

Of course, if we are going to be obedient to God, then we have to get back into the practice of listening to him. I heard recently of a man who was had up in court for not speaking to his wife. He had been married to her for five years and during that period he hadn't spoken a word, so she filed divorce proceedings against him. At the end of the proceedings the magistrate, very distraught with what he had heard, turned to the man and said, 'I don't understand how you could treat your wife in such a way, not speaking to her for five years. What have you got to say for yourself?' He replied in sullen tones, 'Well, I didn't like to interrupt....'

I don't know whether God feels the same today about us. He hears a great deal of talking from us, but he certainly does want to interrupt. There are a lot of things that God has to say to us if only we will listen. God is doing an amazing thing in our country, and he is doing it according to his own strategy and his own plan, and if we want to be a part of that then we need to listen carefully—each one of us individually, and corporately in our churches—to what he is saying. 'Jesus is head of the church' must become more than mere words. Having heard what he is saying, however difficult that might be, we have to begin to apply it, if we want to be a part of God's working. There is much said about a 'call to repentance', but repentance has to do with a change of direction in specific areas, not just a general awareness that things aren't right.

I am writing this with two strong feelings. One of great excitement, and the other of deep concern. The excitement is that God is at work and that there is a tremendous sense of expectancy in many places. There is evidence everywhere that the tide is rising! All over the place there are indications of fresh life. Although God has been working in miraculous ways, touching many people's lives, pouring out his Spirit, it has up to this time been in only small measure. It has been like the drops of rain before a storm. For many years God has promised an awakening across this nation, and although it is dangerous to drop into a revival mentality that says we will wait until revival comes tomorrow, and so do nothing today, I believe that many have that sense that rain is in the air. There is certainly a greater hunger in the world amongst unbelievers for spiritual things than there has been for a long time. Many share the same conviction that the 'tide of faith' has turned and that there is a growing interest in the gospel, far greater than for many years. If this is so, the real crisis is over the church's ability to be ready to meet the need and put the net out where the fish are. I am a believer in the need for revival—but evangelism as we know it is insufficient for the needs of the hour.

The deep concern is that the church in Britain today is neither ready nor equipped for either persecution or revival. These two experiences are not mutually exclusive; both could happen together. If the church buildings were closed, the vast majority of Christians would be lost in a wilderness because there is no network of relationships already built up to maintain church life. Our church life is not geared to reaping the potential harvest in front of us. It is frightening to think that we are coming to a time of great opportunity but are not able to respond to it. We must reassemble our lines.

If large numbers of people were to be converted, we would

have serious difficulty coping with them, and a large number would fall away and be lost. I don't believe that that in any way denies the work of the Holy Spirit in keeping people. But you don't make disciples purely by bringing them into the kingdom. They need to be taught and helped, and that takes human involvement.

The church that has its basic structures right can accommodate and disciple any number of new believers and encourage them into discipleship. The potential for growth is in fact limitless. It is possible for us either to limit the moving of the Spirit or to facilitate his work—in both size and quality. If we do not seriously consider the basic principles and structures of our church life, then revival will be like so many of the past: tremendously exciting during a period of outpouring, but limited in its full effect and dead within a generation. If we have revival without restoration, we will have the triumphs and the tragedies of the Welsh revival all over again. We are proving our great ability to run bigger and better conferences, but that could easily become a cover-up for lack of reality at grass roots.

What is being written here is deliberately not illustrated by examples of the successes and failures of what either I am involved in in my own particular neck of the woods or of other people's work. If I were to base it on the failures and triumphs of one fellowship, there would be an immediate attempt by some to copy that. There are tremendously exciting examples of church growth both in denominations and in the new house-churches in different parts of Britain. But it would be wrong to use them as an example. We need to discover basic principles and then apply them in the specific way our unique situation requires and as the Holy Spirit directs.

It is interesting that, in the New Testament, the details of church structure in terms of leadership and eldership are surprisingly vague. There is enough there to indicate the principles on which the church should be founded, but also enough not said in order to enable us to be free to be led by the Spirit in our own particular situation.

This is also true, of course, in the area of worship. The Bible says very little about New Testament worship services. If we were given an outline of what a New Testament service was like, we would all have copied that and repeated it week after week. Then we would be completely trapped in one particular form of worship. The Bible gives principles on which to base our worship. This enables tremendous freedom of the Spirit to work in each given situation. It is the joy of a living body. The structure gives support and enables freedom, and is not hindered by being solid and rigid. It is the basic principles that are important, and the willingness to listen to God, not only for the vision but for the implementation of that vision.

Ready to suffer?

God is calling us to prepare not only for revival, but for suffering. The church in Britain today is in no shape to cope with severe suffering and persecution. A person may consider himself a pillar of the local church, but when the wave of suffering comes, as surely it will, he will be knocked down with the rest if he has not made adequate preparation. The preparation required is both personal and corporate. The personal aspect concerns real repentance at all levels of life, discovering the lordship of Christ and the necessity of being filled with the Holy Spirit. The corporate aspect concerns building your life into the local body of believers by stretching out your hands in close fellowship with those around you. If you know that suffering is coming, you must be prepared. When the Lord shakes the 'heavens and the earth', the only thing that will stand will be the kingdom of God. All that is man-made will fall.

Time for action

Michael Harper in a recent editorial wrote:

> In the last few years there have been a whole spate of films about disasters. Earthquakes, fires, aerial collisions and sinking ships have kept audiences breathless with excitement. But common to all these kinds of films is the fact that the terrifying experiences seem to have a real effect on those involved in the disasters. People who are often complete strangers, gang up in their fight for survival. The instinct for

self-preservation is common to everyone, except, it would seem, Christians! While economic and political disasters surround us, and our churches are weak and spiritually powerless, we still seem to carry on pig-headedly, as if all were well. It is increasingly difficult to see how we can justify the luxury of our independence from each other in the light of the gathering storm.

In these disaster films, people do not have much time to plan anything. They do not form discussion groups or elect a committee. All they can do is to stretch out their hands to the nearest person available. It does not seem much, but when everyone does it, the human chain grows and grows until all are included. This is something we can all do, and, speaking for myself, I want to be doing it more and more in the coming days.

Stretch out your hands

It is these words 'stretch out your hands' that express God's longing and desire for his people today. The effects and repercussions of it will be incalculable. It will be like the connecting up of an electrical circuit, the putting together of pipes in a pipeline, the parts themselves being of little significance—except as channels of power. It is in their coming together that the effectiveness comes and the flow of power is possible. The power is not the circuit or the pipelines themselves, but they provide the vehicle.

If Christians across Britain hold hands with forgiveness, repentance and love in their hearts, the power of God will be able to flow with unbelievable speed and strength.

The greatest (but not the only) barrier to this is the ministers and leaders in the church. In this hour of need, why do people insist on remaining apart instead of joining hands in love and fellowship?

We do not live in the days of Wesley, Moody or Jonathan Edwards, even though there are many parallels; we live in an age of renewal in the church. There are plenty around who want to be God's answer to Britain, but although God does use evangelists and prophets, he is wanting to use an army of people rather than a single person.

It's been interesting to notice the marvellous response that there has been to the tragic yet gloriously triumphant story of Joni. It has been amazing to see the way God has been able to shine through her and to enable her. But for a person to fully express himself, a body in full working order is required. The body of Christ in Britain is crippled, paralysed, deformed and divided. We have had to learn to do everything with our mouths! We have become a word-oriented church, headed up by individuals with the ability to speak. Jesus wants to work through a body! Why should he be denied it! He died to produce a united, healed and cleansed body. He sent the Holy Spirit to empower a united body. He is coming again for a united body, his bride. How long will we go on pandering to our egos in order to prevent his body being healed? What is needed in Britain today is a body movement, a people movement, a vast army of men and women holding hands and marching for God.

Holding hands

Have you noticed in a meeting, if someone says 'Let's hold hands', you just take the hand of the person next to you? You don't stop to ask him his background, his church affiliation, and his views on baptism! You accept him as a brother and hold his hand. What a tragedy it would be if everyone suddenly moved around the hall to find someone they liked holding hands with!

God is saying to you and me, sitting in our homes, 'Hold hands with those next to you.' Unity is not cheap. For many it will be costly if it is to be any more than a super-spiritual unity, which is all words and hugs and no reality. To some it will mean the pain of forgiveness and repentance from resentment and bitterness. For others, particularly leaders, it will be a surrender of their ego and pride. For some it will sadly mean criticism and antagonism from their fellow brethren. For God it will mean the availability of an extremely powerful instrument in his hand to reach the world.

It cost Jesus his life to make us one! What will you and I pay to maintain that unity? Unity between people, not institutions or structures, unity that will bring about a renewed vehicle for God's use.

2

Forget the former things

'The wind is changing direction' is really the best way to summarize many people's assessment of the situation in the church over the past two or three years following a tremendous period of renewal and refreshment. Something different seems to be happening. When the wind changes the sailor has to retrim his sails to produce maximum speed. It's possible to look back over the last few decades and discern definite moves and patterns in the workings of God in this country, and they are evidence that God is not finished with this nation.

For the people of God, those who have been looking to God to lead and direct them, there always comes a time for moving on. Such times are always both difficult and exciting, because they are times of conflict as well as advance and opportunity.

Despair

I remember so clearly being filled with a tremendous sense of despair for months on end in the summer of 1980, as I thought about all that had happened in the last few years in Britain. I had seen so many Christians come alive in the Spirit, discovering new vitality in worship and praise. I had seen the euphoria and excitement of large gatherings of Christians and a growing sense that something tremendous was about to happen. And I remember thinking of all the promises that God had given of bringing revival to this nation, and being so excited to see just the beginnings of it taking place in the church.

And yet the momentum of the charismatic movement (as people called it) seemed to be dying down, and many people were saying it had come to an end. Disillusionment was beginning to set in. Many people had really believed that God was going to renew their fellowships, but now they were beginning to wonder if it would ever really happen. People were getting frustrated.

I found myself asking the questions that I think many people were asking but probably not daring to voice publicly. 'What has actually been achieved? Have we got any closer to making an impact on Britain; after all that has happened, is there really nothing to show for it? So much has been going on and yet so little seems to have happened; there is so little to see.' In the midst of this despair and disillusionment God spoke to me through a daily reading in the book of Zechariah. In a nutshell what he said was that the thing about foundations is that you've got nothing to show for them at the end of the day if—you only judge by what you see. And God was saying that what he had been doing was building foundations!

He had been touching the lives of thousands of Christians and renewing them *individually*. He had been developing links between men and women across the country that he intended to use. He had been preparing leaders and training them for the task ahead. He had been placing men and women strategically where he wanted them. I felt he was showing me that he was about to start work on the visible building. And it wasn't going to be by men's ability or men's strength; it was to be a sovereign work of his Spirit. I presumed he meant that he was about to do a great deal of evangelism, but now I believe he was saying something very much more than that, that he was actually going to form a church that was strong, a church that he could use in reaching vast numbers of people. Everyone seemed to be getting excited about evangelistic projects, but so much of it had the marks of man's initiative and man's planning about it; God was into something different.

I believe, too, that what has in the most part been contained within the established structures will soon break out in every direction. It is not a question of 'stay in' or 'come out', but *reform*. A new re-formation was to take place.

19

The new work of God is not going to be constructed on the framework of denominationalism but on the basis of the ministries of men and women God has put in his church, and on the formation of new expressions of the body of Christ in each place. What is expressed in the following pages is a belief that God is preparing a new wineskin to catch the wine. It is also his means of 'thrusting out' labourers to bring in the harvest.

Surfing for beginners

To change the metaphor, it has often been noted that the workings of God come in waves. They are very similar to the waves on the seashore. There is a build-up, a breaking, and then a spreading out. If you look back across the last few years, you can see the waves that have broken in Britain. Right through the seventies there was a very obvious movement of God which was like a wave breaking across the country. There are many people today who have a sense of frustration and a longing for more to happen: could it in fact be just the still before the next wave? If you ever go surfing, you often feel a bit silly standing with the water up to your waist, holding your surf-board, apparently doing nothing. But if you are really wanting to be brought in by the wave, then you have to wait for the right moment. The priority, then, is to be ready. You have to be careful not to go in before the wave comes. But you also have to be careful that you don't miss the wave. So often when people surf, they get caught by surprise because the big breaker comes and they miss it. The priority today is to be ready for the next great wave.

Being ready does not denote inactivity. Often preparation is a time of great activity, but it is as much a response to God as anything else. It requires listening quietly to what God is saying and then being prepared to go out and obey. If a guest is coming to visit you, you prepare beforehand.

Many people know the tremendous exhilaration and sense of power there is in being pushed along by a wave on a surf-board when you time it exactly right, and that is what God longs for each one of us—that we will ride in the power and the stream of his Holy Spirit, being obedient to him. But if there is another wave coming it is fatal to stand around admiring the scenery. We need to be ready.

All that's been happening over the past years has been preparation for what God still intends to do. The tremendous movement during the 1954 Billy Graham Harringay Crusades launched a whole new generation of evangelical leadership across the country, the fruit of which was not fully seen for about ten years. The growth of evangelicalism, particularly in the Anglican Church, owes a great deal to that period.

Since then, beginning in the 1960s, the charismatic movement has grown and has permeated every sector of church life and tradition. In many cases the evangelicals have found it hardest to embrace. The Holy Spirit has been bringing new life and power to many individuals, and in some cases to whole fellowships, with new understanding and experience of worship and gifts of the Spirit. Intermingled with this, we have seen the Festival of Light and the Jesus Movement in the early seventies, the prophetic ministry of *Come Together*, the proliferation of camps and conferences, regionalized praise rallies, city-wide celebrations of faith, and a whole host of other things that have stirred and encouraged the faith of Christians up and down the country. The list is endless, but each has been given by God to strengthen the church.

All this has predominantly been at an individual level. Then, often through frustration, many people have come out of the denominational churches and formed new house-churches. There has been a vast proliferation of these new fellowships throughout Britain. These have been an indication, a forerunner if you like, of something new that God is doing in the country in preparation for a far greater work.

But the wind is changing. And the word for today is, *forget the former things, do not dwell in the past. For I am doing a new thing. Do you not perceive it?* We are at a crisis point. There are many today who desire to listen and respond to God. But it is going to be as hard for them—even those involved in the charismatic movement—to move into God's new thing as it was for many evangelical Christians to accept a new move of the Spirit. If we want to see God building his church in this nation, and to

21

experience revival which will turn Britain upside down and inside out, then we must respond to God's call today.

1. Forget the former things

Tired by failure

Many are unable to move forward because of the failures and disappointments of the past. Many are tired, weary and discouraged. They feel like Peter, who had been out all night and caught nothing. Jesus told him to put down his net and everything in him said there was no point. He had tried every idea in the book and had had enough.

But if Peter had allowed his sense of personal failure, his tiredness, his experienced assessment of the situation based on years of fishing, to prevail, he would have missed the most exciting miracle. When it happened, he knew it wasn't his ability or his skill that had done it. He knew it was the Lord. But it came through obedience and a willingness to look a fool, a willingness to die to himself. Coming to the end of yourself is often the beginning of a whole new world. A world of faith.

Trapped by blessing

Many are trapped by the blessings of the past. We cling to yesterday's manna although we are aware that it is turning sour on us. We want to recapture the excitement and thrill of what we have experienced. We have seen a particular result and so we repeat it ad nauseam, to get the same blessing. There is a nostalgia that creeps in that is totally unbelieving in a God who is alive and active. We see it so clearly in many organizations and events which are born of the Spirit but which nobody has the courage to stop when the Spirit has finished using that particular channel. We have a wonderful ability to start new things but a total inability to stop them. The Fountain Trust showed unique courage. It's time a lot more people dared to stop what they started. Of course people will protest because they were blessed by that, but that is no reason to keep things going for ever. Usually human ego and security are so wrapped up in these institutions that we cannot afford to let them die.

You have seen God at work in the past through particular people and certain situations. Are you willing to forget them? Of course you must learn from experience, but you must not be led by it. Some (though not all) of the desire to see Billy Graham back in Britain to lead a major national crusade has been nostalgia. People whose heart's desire is to see effective evangelism in Britain, and their only remembrance of that is through Billy Graham. Their longing is right, but could it be that God could do a new thing? He may well choose to use Billy Graham, but not necessarily in the same way as before. That in no way denies the vital part large-scale evangelism has to play, nor the tremendous ministry God has given to Billy Graham. (Personally, I am very excited by his proposed visit to this country, but I pray it will be seen in the context of a wider ministry.) Can we forget the former things, both the failures and the successes?

Tied by tradition

Traditions that have grown up because they have been a very helpful means of blessing in the past can be the most terrible blockage to God moving in a church in the present. Every time people want to obey God and move in new ways and new directions, they hit the same barriers of church tradition. Nehemiah's builders were hindered by 'much rubble' and the same rubble of past traditions is a vast stumbling block that needs to be cleared out of the way. In times of deadness, traditions are clung to as they offer security. But you cannot launch a boat out into the deep that will not untie from the jetty, nor lift its anchor.

2. Do not dwell in the past

God continually reminded the children of Israel of his dealings with them. Their feasts and special days were to remind them of his faithful provision. But the purpose of remembrance was to be a spur to faith in the future. Remember all that God has done. Rejoice in it. Thank him for it. It will build faith. But beware of being nostalgic and dreaming of some bygone day when God was 'really with you'. In fact if you could be transferred back then, you would probably find the reality of the situation quite different from the dream.

3. For I am doing a new thing

It is God that is doing a new thing. It isn't that we have to strive for it, or organize it, but we have to co-operate with him. The problem with new things is that they are new! You can't conjecture with your mind what they are unless God reveals it to you. Everybody assumed that the new phase for the eighties was evangelism and so the whole world has gone bananas on evangelism, but in fact very few people are actually doing it and being effective. Of course God's purpose in what he is doing is to reach the lost, but he is doing it in his own way. He is far more concerned about reaching the world than we are. Take another look at the cross if you need reminding.

We must be very careful not to presume but rather listen to what he is saying, because our ways are so superficial and inadequate compared with his. Are we willing to join with God in a new thing? Are we willing to be pioneers? New things are unbelievably hard to associate with. When you have fought hard to stand for a position taking ground with God, it is easy to become entrenched. The new command to move forward is then surprisingly difficult. Spiritual grasshoppers find it quite easy because they hop from one thing to another achieving very little. Those who have fought for truth and made a stand as pioneers easily become settlers!

If we rush today into superficial evangelism, we shall not achieve what God intends for this country—and that is to make a deep effective change upon the whole nation which will have far wider effects than within these shores. First of all we must see what God is doing in the church, and it is through what he is doing in the church, in building bodies for himself, that we will see how much more effective and long-lasting his means of evangelism is.

24

4. Now it springs forth

In other words, it's already happening. And it is! God is doing it. No committee has organized it. (And no committee can stop it.) No individual has invented it. No organization has promoted it. No millionaire has sponsored it. God is doing it. You can't stop it but you can join it. The tide is rising—get your swimming gear on!

5. Do you not perceive it?

It is possible for God to be doing this new work and for us not to see it. We may be looking in the wrong direction. Do you see it? It may not be to your liking, according to what you feel ought to happen. It may not promote you or your work. But do you see it? Look around and ask yourself what is happening that is new? If you look about you will see the very clear evidence that God is doing something new. All over the place something very exciting is happening. Do you see it in the home groups that are springing up; do you see it in the new churches that are forming; do you see it in the old ones that are re-forming; do you see what God is doing?

6. What is God's purpose?

'I will make a way in the wilderness, rivers in the desert'—and isn't that exactly what we have all been praying for? How will God revive the wilderness of his church? Even more important, how will he ever reach the wilderness of Britain for Christ? It's so barren, so dry and resistant to the gospel. What of the massive housing estates, the factories, the unemployed. But what a promise! '*I* will make a way in the desert.' God will do it.

Judgement or blessing

There is absolutely no doubt that Britain is a nation under the judgement of God. We are experiencing in our national life the fruits of godlessness. In our pride, arrogance and greed we have rejected the Christian basis to our corporate and individual life, and all that is happening around us is evidence of God's anger.

But God's judgement is intended to bring us to repentance. He has spared us, until this point in time, from overthrow by a foreign power, although we are all aware that this could happen very suddenly and comparatively easily.

Repentance must begin in the church. A vague call to repentance which many are giving today sounds authentic, but repentance means *change*. If God is speaking to his church and calling them to repentance, then there must be specific action that he requires. If we do not respond to God today we have only ourselves to blame for the very severe consequences that will surely follow.

Can you see in the economic and social problems of Britain the hand of a loving God? The recessions, the unemployment, inflation, the nuclear threat and all the enormous difficulties that have gone with these? What have they achieved? They have created the best environment for preaching good news for a very long time. When people have 'never had it so good' they aren't so interested in Christ. But when the man in the street sees all his props falling under him, he begins to search and ask questions.

Now look what is happening alongside this great shaking and disquiet. God is preparing a church to reach a desperate world. The world is increasingly ready to hear. But it is not just listening to words, it is looking for reality. The church must be ready to be used, but it's going to require a radical and dramatic change (although a very simple one) if the church is going to be ready to meet the needs of this hour.

It could happen very quickly if we will only respond. We are experiencing renewal. We have been praying for revival. God is calling us to reformation within the church to produce a reaping in the world. For it is when the world experiences the great shaking of God that everything that is not of the kingdom of God falls. Then men and women will look around to find something that is stable, and the only thing that is stable is the kingdom of God. The kingdom of God—not represented inside a church building, but lived out in the everyday lives of ordinary Christian people. Our church life today is not stable. But if we start to build a kingdom in reality in the local areas in which we live, then we will have something that the world is looking for and to which the world can come running. God will have an instrument that does not rely upon gimmicks or organization, but is available for his power to flow through.

God will move and God will move in power, and he will move where there are channels available for him to move. The tragedy is that so many have entrenched themselves into such fixed positions that God will have to bypass them in any fresh work that he is doing.

I was in a town recently when God gave a very clear word to a group of evangelical Christians who refused to be open to what God was doing through the gifts of his Spirit and ministries in the church. They had dug themselves in. God's message to them was that he would bypass them if they didn't respond! For God is going to reach a needy world which is crying out to him, and if we in our stubbornness refuse to obey him, then he will have to work in a new way to reach the lost. What a tragedy that will be for so many of us.

3

Jesus weeps for his church

God has feelings too! He has deep, deep feelings. It is time we began to ask ourselves what God feels about his world and about his church. Here we would find a motivation far beyond that given by pure statistics or clinical facts. We so often talk to God about our concern for evangelism, as if he had to be persuaded of its importance. God sees the reality of the glory of heaven and the horror of hell. We have drifted away from teaching about hell for fear of being labelled as 'fire and brimstone' preachers. But to know in your heart of the certainty of hell provides an enormous drive to tell people of Christ.

You only have to look at the cross to see the depth of God's feelings for men and women. How does God feel when he looks down upon a world of men and women wandering around lost and looking for reality and purpose? He knows that he has done everything possible to provide for their needs. How did the father feel as he thought of his son in the far country? Can you imagine the longing in his eyes as he came looking?

Then he looks at his church, the instrument that he has called to proclaim the good news, and he sees people like small children fighting one another, and arguing over petty things. He gives us gifts and all we can do is quarrel over them. Prayer meetings are so often concerned with personal self-centred needs that vary in content from holidays to healing. Of course he is concerned with our needs, but how often must he cry out, 'Does anybody care about my world and the millions who are lost?' He listens in on PCC meetings and elders' meetings in churches and finds them continually discussing issues to do with buildings, spending hours and hours of time and energy in petty matters to do with the fabric, raising money, and the organization of godless schemes, as if these were the hub of church life, when there are thousands of people around them who are hungry for God and no one really seems to care.

He sees men, filled with his Spirit, set against each other, protecting their work and their particular movement. The church has splintered into a vast number of small groups each thinking it has a monopoly on God and his truth. He sees a people divided by petty doctrinal issues instead of united by his life and power, loving one another despite their differences of emphasis and teaching. He looks for a people united against a common enemy, and finds a people weakened and limping through division.

What an indictment it is to discover that a major reason people have rejected Christianity (this is particularly true of young people) is because of what they have seen of the church. In the main, its services are dull, outdated, lifeless and unfriendly, and its message has nothing to say to people's real lives. 'Jesus is alive' on the notice board outside is denied by everything that happens within.

Grief

Can you imagine the sense of sheer frustration and grief that God feels when he looks at his church? When Nehemiah returned to rebuild the walls of Jerusalem, his motivation did not come because he was bored and thought rebuilding would give him something to do! Nor did he academically assess the facts: 'The walls are down and it would be a good thing if at some stage they could be rebuilt!' When he heard the news concerning Jerusalem, he felt what God felt. He knew the shame that there was in the city of God being in ruins. It was a city that was supposed to speak of God's power and glory, of his protection and provision for his people, and it was in total disarray. The agony of it! No wonder he began to weep and to cry. His heart was stirred to the very deepest level.

People today are not moved to evangelism by statistics of the amount of lost people; they are moved first in their hearts by the love of God, feeling what he feels for needy people in the world. The same is true with the needs of the church. We will not today start to deal with the sin and the problems of the church because someone does a time and motion study and produces a report, or because someone comes up with statistics to show what we are really like. We will be moved when we feel God's deep sadness—and his burning anger—at much of what he sees in his church.

Nehemiah heard that the wall around Jerusalem was broken down. Today the church has been so compromised, there is no wall that distinguishes it from the world. It allows all the corruption and evil of society to adulterate it at every level. He heard that the gates were destroyed. Today the gates of the church, symbolizing the basic support systems of church life, are almost non-existent.

Nehemiah wept. Then he prayed. He didn't pray prayers of condemnation, nor did he wallow in guilt. He acknowledged that the mess they were in was due to their own sin, and he recognized that he was fully identified with that. *Don't point the finger at the church. You are part of it!* We are in a mess because of our corporate sin. There is only one answer to that, and that is to acknowledge and confess our sin and receive God's forgiveness for the church of which we are all a part.

Then Nehemiah got to work.

If you feel what God feels for his people, don't sit in arrogant superiority, but weep with him for his people that the whole church will be restored. Then begin to work.

Adultery

In the past, when God wanted to show his people how he felt, he would describe it in terms of a human emotion that we can understand. I suppose one of the most painful things for a man to experience is to fall deeply in love with a woman and then to find that she is committing adultery with somebody else. I am sure most men, even if they have not actually experienced that, know the depth of pain that that would cause them.

I remember talking to a girl who had fallen deeply in love with a young man. After a period of time they got married. Shortly after that, her husband's best friend began visiting the house during the day when her husband was out at work. She spent time with him and went back to his flat. After three months of marriage she was spending her days with this man, going to bed with him, and in the evening playing the loving wife. Then he found out! It took him years to recover from the pain and hurt, for he loved her very deeply.

Again and again in the Old Testament, God talks about his bride—his church—as a harlot, in terms of someone who has committed adultery. You only have to read the prophecy of Hosea to get the depth of God's feelings for his people. Read again Ezekiel 16. He talks about a child who grows up to be a beautiful woman, upon whom he has bestowed undeserved favour, with all sorts of wonderful things. Then this woman turns her back upon the one who has given her everything. 'But you trusted in your beauty and played the harlot.' There God is revealing something of the depth of his feelings for his people. How can you read that passage and fail to be moved? If you truly love God, you will be stirred by knowing something of how he feels.

Listen to this familiar love song (Is 5:1–4):

> My beloved had a vineyard on a very fertile hill.
> He digged it and cleared it of stones,
> And planted it with choice vines;
> He built a watchtower in the midst of it,
> And hewed out a wine vat in it;
> And he looked for it to yield grapes,
> But it yielded wild grapes.
>
> Judge, I pray you, between me and my vineyard.
> What more was there to do for my vineyard,
> That I have not done in it?

What more could God do for his church that he has not done? But it is full of bitter fruit, unpleasant to the world around.

If we know that God feels this way, then how can we continue to do the things that we know cause God any grief? How can we

31

continue to behave in such a way that God feels this sense of agony and pain? It is not that we are to feel sorry for God. But we should share his feelings.

A friend of mine had set aside time for prayer concerning his local area. He asked God to show him what he felt about his body the church in that locality—at which point he began to cry. He is not an over-emotional person, but he found himself weeping uncontrollably with deep sobs. He said he could neither sit nor stand, but walked around not knowing what to do with himself for nearly an hour, until the crying abated. He felt very strongly that the word that best described the church was *fragmented*. He commented later, 'I never knew God felt like that.'

Another friend, living nearby, came to see me later, and said that as he had been praying, God had spoken to him again and again of his desire for what he wanted to do in that area. 'I long for a body in this place through which I can express myself.' In that area there are lots of 'churches' and lots of Christians. So what was wrong? Christ's body was in total disarray and nobody seemed aware of it or appeared to care.

Disunity

When God looks down on a village, town or area of a city, what does he see? He sees his people, his body in that locality, however small or however large. It is made up of all believers. He has put them in that place. That is his local body, his church. It is the instrument through which he wishes to express himself. But in almost every case, the local body is in disarray and disunity.

This is typified by what happens on a Sunday morning in most places where there are a lot of Christians living. In the same street you will see Christians coming out of their front doors, some to walk to the Anglican church, some to walk to the Baptist church, others to the United Reformed church, and a number to the newly-formed house church and so on. Then many others will get in their car and drive several miles to a live church on the other side of town, or even further. Tragically this situation is rarely rectified by differing approaches during the week. What on earth is going on!

Commuter Christians

In so many cases people are unable to get involved in their local area because they 'go to church' (an expression that underlines the problem) outside that locality. They cannot get involved in church life because they do not live close enough to do so. In fact their real effectiveness is completely neutralized, but they usually fill their lives with enough activity to hide the fact. What is actually happening is that while people in reality belong to the church in the area in which they live, they travel each week to another place and therefore to another church. They are trying to belong to two local groups of Christians at once, and usually not being effective in either. The trouble is that it enables Christians to avoid real involvement with the world in either place and so destroys their effectiveness. Surely we need to be in a situation where, as we shop in the supermarket, wait at the bus stop, or collect the children from the school, we will naturally meet other members of our church—and the people outside the church that we are called to reach. We must have this day-by-day contact with the community that God has put us in.

Community life

We live in a society in which community spirit is very nearly lost in most places. There are a variety of factors that have brought this about. One of these is the sad fact that people are continually moving for their job, and so never really settle anywhere for long. Another is television, which makes people very insular and self-contained. The average person will be hard pressed to tell you anything about his neighbours or the people living in the same road. In most suburban areas the majority of people rarely walk down their road—they drive. That's not conducive to meeting people. The pub has probably been the greatest factor in maintaining community life. Not the church.

There is no doubt that this breakdown in community life, that was so strong in the terraced streets of our inner-city areas, is having a severely detrimental effect on society as a whole. Problems such as loneliness and fear are vastly increased. The tragedy is that the living church has failed to be a stabilizing influence in society, as it has the same commuter spirit that there is in society at large. We live in one place, work in another and worship in another. The church, in the real sense of that word, should actually be holding a community together, because it consists of a people who form a network of relationships in that local area, provide initiative for community events, and are known to be the secure element in the locality. Can you imagine what would happen if a law was passed that no one was allowed to drive their car on a Sunday! Our whole church life would be revolutionized.

There is a strong feeling in many places that the employment situation, the whole future of the nature of work, will force people back into their communities, and the local community will again become the centre of people's lives. Micro-chip technology has its effect on business techniques and education; it tends to make people more and more insular and introverted. This can already be seen in games such as space invaders, children's computer games and home video. The Christian has a growing responsibility to get in there amongst people, not to maintain middle class Christian values often mistakenly interpreted as New Testament Christianity, but to encourage Christian attitudes to life and the value of human relationships based on loving and caring.

We often quote the verse, 'By this all men will know that you are my disciples, if you have love for one another' (Jn 13:35). We assume we achieve this when we have reached the dizzy heights of liberation and hug each other in church. But the world never sees that! What it would see and be amazed at is people of different backgrounds who live close to each other caring for each other in practical and meaningful ways, ways that express more than just friendship. The love that Jesus talked about is supernatural. Anyone can love a friend, but real love is towards those we don't normally relate to. It isn't to do with feelings either. It's to do with giving and sacrifice.

Every street

These same people who learn to love one another would soon become aware of the needs around them. Wouldn't it be exciting if in every street in Britain there were a group of Christians who met, prayed together and met the needs of those around? Then the world would see and believe. An exciting concept, but concepts only become reality when people begin to take the plunge and get involved. It's no good saying that that's a nice idea unless you and I have the courage to put it into practice. It's far easier to go to church on Sunday than to go out of your way to meet the neighbours.

Local church?

How often do we find ourselves saying, 'What church do you go to?' or talking about 'my church' or 'your church' or 'so and so's church'. *If you live in a place, you are part of the body of Christ in that area, whether you like it or not.* It does not really matter if it is your sort of church, or whether they are the sort of people you like. You belong to the church in that area.

In most local areas, there will be a number of denominational churches, none of which will be fully representative of the body of Christ; each will contain parts of it. The group of believers that you relate to must never be on the basis of denomination. The question you must ask is, Which church gives the best opportunity to be part of the local body of believers? There is no reason why there should not be several 'churches' in an area, provided they recognize themselves to be part of *one local church*, meeting separately because of numerical convenience rather than denominational loyalty. If this is not the situation there is a strong case for a new expression of the body to begin, which gives better opportunity to show life. This would be alongside but not necessarily separate from what already exists. More of that later!

Each of us belongs to the church in the area in which we live. In most cases, a locality is fairly easily defined by the community around you and will consist of what is reasonable walking distance. Of course, this may not be true of country areas. You cannot pick and choose which church you belong to. You belong to the local body and Christ has given gifts and ministry to the body. We'll only discover this if we see the church as *local and geographical, not denominational*. The local church consists of all those that have the Spirit of Christ and know Christ as Saviour and Lord. The word 'church' is used in Scripture both for the entire local body of believers in a place and for the smaller groupings within that. But the smaller groupings in the early church considered themselves all to be a part of the larger whole and were meeting in homes purely out of numerical convenience. Paul was angry if it were for any other reason, like 'I'm of Apollos, I'm of Paul'.

Entrenched in tradition

We are so entrenched in our thinking about the church that the concept I am suggesting is to most of us revolutionary and upsetting; it needs to be grasped carefully. The key is that you belong where you are. There's a poster around that says 'Bloom where you are planted'. God put you there for a purpose; you belong to the body in your locality. You may say, 'Well, there aren't many Christians in my area.' If you keep going away, then there aren't going to be any at all! Maybe God put you there because there weren't many others. What good is salt in a salt cellar? Many thriving churches today have a large 'floating' element in the congregation who come in from outside. The word to them is, 'Go back where you belong.' That's not intended to be harsh, but it is the only way people will really find their place. Nor is it intended to be a hard and fast rule, as there will always be exceptions. We should be driven by conviction rather than a sense of guilt.

God is surely grieved at our denial of his body. People flock from many different local communities to one particular place, and the place in which they live is denuded of any effective witness. What will you and I do about it? If you see that it is true, you cannot just put your head in the sand and believe it doesn't apply to you. For God's sake and for the sake of a dying world, we must not run away!

Convenient Christianity

Not only do people travel out of their locality in order to go to church and therefore deny the whole concept of the local body of Christ, but also within any given locality there is usually a whole cluster of groups that call themselves churches, but their reason for division is denominational and not geographical. There's seldom any real unity. If, in the Lord's eyes, there is only one church in any given locality, these are only fragmented expressions of the church, or at best separated congregations of the one church. If the latter is the case, it must be recognized as such. The leaders need to be of one heart and mind if there is to be effectiveness in the area. Watchman Nee, the great Chinese saint, had this to say:

> Many people think it is good to have denominations. Do you know why? Because it is convenient. Brothers! If you ask me according to the flesh whether or not I like denominations, I would say, yes I like them, because everything is clear cut. Those who like to speak in tongues can go to the tongues church, those who like independent congregations can go to the congregational church, those who like baptism by sprinkling can go to the church that practises that, but the Bible teaches that in each locality there should only be one church. This way it is not so convenient because everyone must love all kinds of brothers! To love my brothers who are unlike me causes much friction and many lessons. You have your proposals and I have my proposals, you have your ideas and I have mine. It is very convenient for you to have your church and me to have my church. It is not convenient for us to be together in one church to love one another. With the many difficulties there are many lessons, with more difficulties there is more love of one another. Even though we are unhappy with each other we still can't escape. Whether we like it or not, we still must be brothers together. You must overcome the carnal ones by the spiritual ones, conquer all differences by love, and conquer all difficulties by grace. Otherwise the church can never be established. [*Further Talks on Church Life,* The Stream Publishers 1969.]

Now I realize that many would disagree with Watchman Nee's dogmatic statement that there is only one church in one city. But when Paul wrote to the Romans, he wrote 'to all God's beloved in Rome who are called to be saints'. Was the church in the houses of Aquila and Prisca (1 Cor 16:19 and Rom 16:5) *the* church in Rome or *a* church in Rome? Was the church in the house of Nympha the same as the church in Laodicea?

The confusion arises over the word 'church'. The word *ekklesia* means those 'called out', or in other words the redeemed community. This is used in the universal sense of the worldwide company of believers, in the sense of the local gathering of Christians, and of a small group of people committed to one another meeting in a house. There is a sense in which a 'cell group' is a church. But it is the coming together of cell groups in an area under an administration of eldership that constitutes a congregation, a local church. I believe that this congregation is the local body of Christ into which he has given gifts and ministries. The unity that Christ longs for is one congregation in one place, which constitutes all those that acknowledge Jesus as Lord and Saviour in their lives.

Most cities today consist of small towns or villages that have come together, each of which has its own community. A local community is often a good boundary for a local church. In a city like Birmingham, although there should be the regular coming together of the people of God, in reality there are a vast number of local churches, because it is made up of a mass of local communities.

So the heart of the matter is that if there is to be division it must be on the basis of *geography*, not *denomination*.

Putting the clock back

We also have to recognize that we don't live in the first century. We live at a time when two thousand years of Christianity lie behind us. We can't suddenly pretend that all that now exists doesn't exist. But we must not be afraid to be radical if we are to be effective in our generation. We must therefore go back to the first principles and see how those principles can be worked out in our present situation. I believe we can rediscover a New Testament experience of church life in a twentieth-century context. The question is not to do with the ability, but with the will and the desire. And if we don't get back to these principles, we will become an irrelevance in our world!

Leaders

The tragedy is that disunity is most clearly seen in the leaders. The reason for this will be discussed later, but the trouble lies primarily in their failure to want to build together the kingdom of God. There is a growing unity among believers today which is denied real expression, and sadly the blockage is among the shepherds (that is the leaders).

God is grieved even by those who are so-called 'moving on with God'. Blessing is not always a sign of God's approval, as we live in a time of blessing. He will work where he sees faith and openness, but it would be foolish to believe that because you are experiencing the blessing of God on your work and church, all is well. There are places where two so-called churches are almost next to each other and being blessed by God, but God is still grieved by the disunity that he sees between them.

In Ezekiel 34 God expresses in no uncertain terms his displeasure at the shepherds of Israel, that is those who have been put in charge of the flock. He talks about how they have exploited the sheep, and have used their position for their own ends. He shows how they have neglected to care for the real needs of people. He talks about how the shepherds have abandoned the sheep and the sheep are scattered, for there is no real care for them.

As you read these chapters you feel something of God's anger towards the shepherds. Isn't that same anger being expressed today towards those who have been put in positions of responsibility and have misused it, however unknowingly? Have you noticed how many churches flourish during an interregnum? (A revealing term in itself. There must be a moral there!)

Unity

Jesus prayed that we might be one. Jesus died on the cross to make it possible for us to be one. Jesus sent his Holy Spirit to give us the power to be one. Jesus longs for his people to be one, not just in a 'spiritual' sense of unity, but in reality. If the world were to end today, and we were all taken to heaven, we would be perfectly and wholly united—so why can't we be united now? What is there that is so different now that will be removed when we are in heaven? Maybe the answer is complex, but certainly one of the answers is *sin*. Sin requires repentance, and repentance means action, or it is not repentance at all.

We need to make a clear distinction between denominational, institutional unity and the unity of the body of Christ. Unity of the former kind is merely academic as far as the real issue is concerned. If the institutional structures are man-made and encompass as many unbelievers as believers, then bringing them together isn't going to change anything. What we need to be concerned about is unity at the local immediate level between people of faith, and not merely organizations. If it is going to be real it must be real where we live.

Sacrifice

Real unity can only be achieved through sacrifice. The greatest barrier today to our coming together is that most of us believe in the concept of unity, but it is unity on our terms! Real unity only comes through willingness to die. The only way that sugar can become united with a cup of tea and actually affect the cup of tea is by being completely dissolved in it. If I really believe that God wants us to be one, then I will be willing for my work, my church, my fellowship to be lost in someone else's work in order that the unity of the body may be attained or surpassed. That doesn't mean that I should compromise the truth, for truth must never be sacrificed. But it does mean that I shall long to see God's heart pleased by seeing his people one. Many, including the majority of clergy, will have to sacrifice denominational allegiance and maintenance of clerical status.

Differences of doctrine, other than on foundational issues of salvation, should never divide us, and yet there are great rifts even between the new house church groups on such issues. Nobody has a monopoly on the truth, but pride tells people otherwise. Doctrine other than that which is foundational can never be the basis of unity. Unity is in Christ alone.

Denominationalism

The Bible talks about the church in the locality. It never talks about the national or state church. Most denominational groups have been formed by dividing away from the mainstream of institutionalized church life. They began with people who thought that God was revealing fresh direction and underlining a need for purity of doctrine and faith, and they could no longer grow within the existing structures. The latest in this line has been the so called house-church movement (in fact most of these meet in schools!). In many cases because of the apparent necessity for national links this has all the makings of a new variety of denomination. These new churches must be open to the possibility that they are not an end in themselves but merely a step along the road to something further that God wants to do. However, this attitude becomes much more difficult if the national links develop too firmly.

Of course there are vast numbers of independent house churches as well as those that form the national networks. This breaking away seems to have been the church's natural way of preserving life over the centuries. Many of the new churches today have clearly been brought into existence by God. A few, sadly, seem to be the product of frustration and an unwillingness to listen to others around them.

The Lord is bringing life to people in all the denominations, which means that there is as much life within the denominations as outside. If God is moving in this way, then we need to work with him in allowing these people to find local expressions of unity that is not merely institutional and therefore hollow. To form a new church in a locality can either aid in the unity of the body or it can actually increase the division. When we look at an area we need to ask ourselves first of all whether or not there is a church, a place where the Bible is believed and taught and the people are open to the work of the Holy Spirit—somewhere the body can find expression. If there is, it is there that we should begin to work and pray.

The sad thing is that many people still cling to their denominational allegiance, even though most of us belong to denominations out of tradition and not conviction. When we move into an area we look for a Baptist church because 'we are Baptists'! But 'I am an Anglican at heart' or 'I am a Methodist really' are expressions of sin, however frivolously they may be said. *Anything that promotes denominationalism, either individually or corporately, is sin and needs to be clearly labelled as such.* If denominationalism is sin, then its only answer is repentance. Repentance is not saying sorry. It is being sorry. That, as I have said, involves action. The genuineness of repentance does not consist in what a man says but in what he does. It is not where you 'go on Sunday' that is at issue, but where your heart is. In fact you could have a living church that never met on Sunday. It is not ideal, but the large meeting should only be a visible expression of something much deeper.

It is not belonging to a denominational church that is wrong. It would be hard not to! But if we make denominational loyalty or methods of worship the main reason for belonging, we are guilty of the sin of denominationalism.

The egg and the bottle

A friend of mine had a recurring dream. He was walking down the road holding an egg in one hand and a bottle in the other. Eventually after some thought he managed to push the egg through the neck of the bottle. Then the egg hatched, and out came a chick that ran up and down inside. It could have walked out but chose not to, feeling secure within the bottle. But it grew and grew, being fed through the neck of the bottle. Eventually it was crushed by the walls of the bottle, unable to move or get out.

The dream spoke to my friend in several ways. It had a personal and a corporate application. There was always the possibility that the hen would break the bottle, but the warning is that the old rigid structure will crush new life, although new life in its early stages finds a degree of freedom and protection in that structure.

The great divide

Evangelical Christians and churches have been known in recent years to boycott events with which Roman Catholics have been involved. If only they knew the pain and grief that that causes to the Lord. Nobody has asked them to identify with the Roman Catholic Church in all its teachings, but simply to walk hand in hand with Catholic brothers and sisters.

Anyone who has experienced the freedom of worship and the depth of prayer and praise expressed by renewed Catholics must realize that they leave most of us Protestants in the nursery in this sphere. They have a great deal to teach us about the awesomeness of God and the joy of loving him, while Protestants have a heritage of biblical teaching to share with them. In fact if renewed Catholics don't turn to a biblical basis of faith they will rely on emotional subjective experience and be susceptible to all kinds of deception.

The heart of the matter is not unity between the Protestant and the Catholic Church structures, but unity among believers, some of whom are Protestants, some of whom are Catholics. If unity is based on belief in justification by faith alone, and the experience of the indwelling of the Holy Spirit, then it will not be a cheap unity. Catholics have got to renounce the belief that the Roman Catholic Church is the only true church. The unity of the Spirit must move towards the unity of faith.

Celebrate the feast

The greatest place for fellowship is around a meal. What a banquet has been arranged for us to celebrate the glorious coming together of Jesus with his bride, the church! A meal made ready for a united people of every race, tribe and tongue. What a glorious and wonderful occasion that is going to be!

Until that day, the Lord has given us another table to sit together around. It is a temporary arrangement. It is both a remembrance of what Christ has done and a preparation for that great day. But it is a table set in a wilderness for us to have fellowship around together, to celebrate as a family in the

43

presence of the Father.

Now feel the grief of Jesus! The Holy Spirit has done a wonderful and precious thing amongst us all. In the Roman Catholic Church, where he has found hearts opened to him, he has been filling, renewing and releasing men and women into a new love and commitment to Jesus. The Holy Spirit has done his work (although it would be wrong automatically to attribute everything in the 'Catholic charismatic movement' to the Holy Spirit). And yet we cannot share the same table!

Is it really that we *cannot*, or that we *will not* share the same table? Surely it isn't purely a matter of doctrinal understanding of the nature of the elements of communion. If we accept and believe that the man next to us who happens to be a Catholic by tradition is also a brother in Christ, how can we continue to grieve that brother, and much more how can we continue to grieve Jesus by not eating with him? Some have two tables. But there aren't two tables, there is only one.

Roman Catholics who have been renewed by the Spirit face the dilemma in the final analysis between the ruling of the church and the leading of the Spirit. Many know in their own hearts the grief of not being able to share together fully with Protestants, but they are waiting for the church to align itself with the same longing of the Spirit that they have in their hearts. But how long can this really continue? I believe that Jesus beckons us to the table to share together. It is the place of reconciliation and the place of healing.

It is even possible that the time will come when renewed Catholics will have to break from the mainstream church. There are many who are at the moment in danger of being compromised doctrinally. The increase in emphasis on the veneration of Mary (as an example), which is apparent in a few places, is certainly causing a lot of serious questions to be asked. The Holy Spirit is the Spirit of truth. There is immense danger in receiving the blessing of the Lord and continuing to embrace falsehood. There must be repentance or things will turn sour.

Could it be that Ezekiel's vision (chapter 37) is relevant now? It is a prophecy concerning two sticks brought together. They represent the two divided kingdoms. One has broken away, but

God's heart had always been to bring them back together, one flock under one shepherd. Many today see it in terms of Jews and Gentiles, but I do believe there is, too, a very real word to Protestants and Catholics. It is not a unity between the Roman Catholic Church and the Church of England, for that will only be an ecclesiastical structural unity (and certainly could never happen without drastic changes in the Roman Catholic Church and deep repentance), but it is a coming together of the people of God from different traditions as one people with one Lord, coming to celebrate with both bread and wine the feast that Jesus provided for us. Let us become peacemakers. The prophet was asked to take a step of obedience and the Lord brought healing and restoration. In heaven we shall be one and sit down at the same table. Why can't we allow the world to see that oneness now?

4

Power, pride and pleasure

Let's look at some of the causes of this inability to discover the body of Christ.

Power

The desire for power and control is insidious but very strong in all of us. It is this desire for power that strangles the church at every level. It is clearly seen as a pattern in the history of the Roman Catholic Church, and although less extreme, it is there in the development of Protestantism as well. It is to be seen in pastors and ministers who want absolute control. It is to be seen in the eldership structures, particularly in the Brethren, and it is there in so many of the new house-churches (and it will be their undoing if they do not determine to root it out). Very often it is not individual power but collective power. A group of men who support each other, whether they be Anglican clergy, Brethren elders, or house-church leaders, start with a vision, but then enjoy the prestige and power which is so often expressed in arrogance and a joyless harshness in their attitude to others. If we do not realize that the potential for power-seeking is in each of us, then we are likely to be deceived. Jesus' call to leaders was to become servants.

Often unity is hailed as a great thing, but as we have mentioned before, it is unity on our terms and there is no real unity without sacrifice. If you enjoy power and desire control, you will never see unity in the body of Christ. How often people have tried to gather together Christians in a given area to express unity, but you will always notice that it is those same people who run the meetings, those people who make the decisions, those people who maintain control. If it is run by one fellowship, other leaders are suspicious and keep their people away. Many clergy prevent their members knowing about other events. They act as censor for their people. That's not service, that's dictatorship.

When God saw the Tower of Babel and observed that men wanted to make a name for themselves, he caused great confusion to come upon them. This confusion came in order for him to save them from themselves. Disunity has often come in breakaway movements, and sometimes strangely enough it is caused by God. God in his goodness, even in recent days, has prevented new power structures being created. Obviously in his eyes disunity is preferable to monolithic power structures. Structures that are based on authority imposed from above and not submission from below will always lead to new popes being created. Jesus wants a body of which he is the head, in which complementary ministries are able to be expressed. He said, 'Whoever would be great among you must be your servant, and whoever would be first among you must be slave of all' (Mk 10:43–44). If anybody wants to be a leader, then he must start by being a servant.

Pride

One of the greatest dangers of any new movement of God, like the house-church movement, will be of elitism and spiritual pride. There is always a danger that we see ourselves as God's chosen instruments. We secretly believe that although he loves his church, he loves one part of it more than the rest! If we are not aware of the potentiality of pride in our hearts, then again we are open to deception.

One of the greatest problems which comes with having a full church is that it can be labelled 'successful'. We measure success by the number of people in the church compared with other churches. How many churches do you know that you call 'alive'? If only we would look realistically and compare the number of people inside with the number of people outside, we would be quickly humbled. In Britain no church could dare call itself successful. (In the Christian life there is no such thing as success and failure, only obedience or disobedience.) No church building should be crammed full Sunday by Sunday, or the congregation will never grow. It may satisfy the ego of those in charge, but it will never satisfy God's heart. A church must divide in order to grow. No home group should permanently run at capacity or it will not grow. It must divide; division with unity.

The church in Britain today is in the main small, powerless, dull and by and large ineffective in reaching the man in the street. Yet paradoxically, pride is one of our major sins. If your fellowship has a name for being alive, then watch out!

Doctrinal pride is another main cause of division. This works on the assumption that one group has received the truth and must separate from another to prevent contamination of its people. How can we allow such arrogance to divide us?

Pleasure-seeking

Why do people travel great distances to church? Why do we like praise meetings and not prayer meetings? Why do people flock from charismatic meetings to conferences and back again?

The answer is pleasure. Some people worship worship. Some worship preachers, others just enjoy sermons. You hear people saying, 'So and so was good last week,' or 'I haven't heard so and so, is he good?' Sermons become something to observe, analyse, criticize and pronounce judgement on. Many even appear to revere the Bible more than the Lord!

Preachers and celebrated ministers can be listened to like pop stars. Isn't it all reminiscent of Ezekiel? Do you remember what the Lord told him?

As for you, son of man, your people who talk together about you . . . say to one another, 'Come, and hear what the word is that comes forth from the Lord.' And they come to you . . . and sit before you as my people, and they hear what you say but they will not do it; for with their lips they show much love, but their heart is set on their gain. *And, lo, you are to them like one who sings love songs* with a beautiful

48

voice and plays well on an instrument, for *they hear what you say, but they will not do it.* When this comes—and come it will!—then they will know that a prophet has been among them. (Ezek 33:30–33.)

Meetings are judged by various criteria, but each one reflects basically whether or not we enjoyed it. We have become a church of pleasure-seekers. We go to meetings for what we can get, and if we don't get it we don't go again but go elsewhere. No wonder there is such pressure to bring in the stars, each one shining brighter than the one before, whether it be a Christian rock group, a healer, a prophet, or an evangelist. Very often it is someone with a breathtaking testimony of a life of debauchery that we can all revel in. The reality of God's goodness in rescuing this person seems to be secondary to the excitement of the things they did before. We don't go to meetings to meet with God any more. He doesn't give us the instant thrills we demand.

How can God mobilize into an army a bunch of comfortable, easy-living, pleasure-seeking idolators? Men of Wesley's day met to seek after holiness and to keep each other close to God's way. Most of us seem to meet when it's convenient and if it's enjoyable.

If a meeting was held in your area for the churches to meet with God, and you found there was to be no speaker, would you go? Usually the first question we ask is, 'Who's speaking?' You try and arrange a meeting without a speaker and people will get all uptight. You dare to have a meeting to meet God and you'll meet God. Somebody will probably in fact speak, but you'll go away knowing you've met the Lord. Most meetings today are arranged so that even if God isn't there, it'll be a good time anyway, and nobody will be disappointed! No wonder God doesn't come in power.

I talked recently to a dear woman who was involved in the Hebredian Revival. She said the great characteristic of the meetings was the tremendous sense of God's presence. Nobody went to hear a great preacher. They went to meet God. And they met him. Everything else paled into the background by comparison. Why not scrap the sermon occasionally and determine to meet God!

Of course our worship should also be enjoyable. So much so that the outsider is struck by its reality and joy. But it will be because God is there. It is amazing how much of a reaction there is to old-fashioned liturgy and how stuck most of us are in our own new liturgy, be it a hymn-prayer sandwich or a charismatic formula. The latter is often even more predictable and, dare I say it, much more superficial than the Anglican liturgy. But freedom needs a framework and the framework needs to allow for freedom. The freedom is for God to have his way with us. We must give him room to move.

Gifts

Isn't it amazing that the issue of spiritual gifts has become so divisive? This is particularly true of 'speaking in tongues'. There is only one important question to be asked: 'Are these gifts from God?' If they are not, have nothing to do with them. If they are, then desire them for your fellowship for all you are worth! You can't be effective without them if God feels it's important for you to have them. Of course there are problems. But would you rather have the quietness, orderliness and predictability of a graveyard, or the problems, joys and vitality of a schoolroom of children who are learning? Let's have life! Let's have clear leadership and order!

Fear

'If we were to do this or change that, what would the people think?' 'It's never been done this way before.' The cry is at the heart of many a pastor or leader. The tragedy is that we do not dare to change and to move forward because of the fear of the people, and often just a few people. We are hindered in doing what is right by a tiny handful of faithful people which in reality prevents thousands of other people being reached for the king-dom of God. We move at the pace of the slowest and therefore are dictated to by the unspiritual.

Strangely enough, it isn't usually the denominational structure that is the first thing to prevent people moving, because most denominations give a far greater degree of freedom at an individual church level than is recognized. It is usually the fear of what the people will think that prevents most pastors from really moving on and obeying God in the way they know to be right. It is the fear of man that is at the heart of the matter. It is closely followed by the fear of losing what we have. We are so geared to a survival mentality that we feel the need to hang on at all costs to what we have got. It is a fear of the unknown, and fear of change. There is great safety and security in treading the well-worn paths and keeping the boat on an even keel.

But faith means being vulnerable, and vulnerability isn't something that we want very much. It is all very well until you face up to the reality of what fear really is. It is the opposite of faith. It is rooted in unbelief and disobedience. Wasn't it these two things that prevented the children of Israel from going into the promised land? And wasn't it expressed in fear? Fear of man, fear of the unknown, fear of failure, fear of their own inability—and what was God's response? He was angry. They saw the promise, they knew the great reward that was in store for them, but they did not really believe his power and they did not believe his love.

Do you remember those devastating words at the beginning of the book of Deuteronomy:

> It is *eleven days' journey* from Horeb by the way of Mount Seir to Kadesh-barnea. And in the *fortieth year,* on the first day of the eleventh month, Moses spoke to the people of Israel....

An eleven-day journey that took forty years because men were afraid through unbelief and disobedience! And we are told that this leads eventually to a disease called 'hardening of the heart'. It's very common today. But there is a remedy. Faith. 'Today when you hear his voice....' Thank God that there is still a today to respond to him.

Much of the leadership in the church today has been guilty of unbelief and disobedience. Many men have even tasted and seen something of what God is doing through renewal and have been aware of what he wanted, but through fear have drawn back. For

51

people to have missed what God is doing today in the church, they would have to be blind. 'What would Mrs Jones think?' is the question they ask. But who is asking 'What would God think?' No wonder the fear of God is the beginning of wisdom. Do you remember how the prophet said 'there is no fear of God in the land'? Unbelief is there at the root of the problem, right through the church.

That may make many feel condemned, but the possibility of change is near at hand. Again the words of Moses in the same discourse inspires them to new faith:

> For this commandment which I command you this day is not too hard for you, neither is it far off. . . . *The word is very near you; it is in your mouth and in your heart, so that you can do it.* [Deut 30:11, 14.]

Unbelief is not only reflected in fear. It is reflected in immorality of every kind. If we believed that God is the God of Moses and Elijah, we would not dare allow our lives to be compromised in the way that they are. The way we allow standards to fall in our behaviour, conversation, business dealings, is evidence of unbelief in God's existence and power.

Sexual immorality is rife in the church. We have allowed the teaching that God is a loving father to dull us into believing that he is unconcerned with sin and that we can do whatever we can get away with. Hear the words of the prophet Amos:

> I hate, I despise your feasts, and I take no delight in your solemn assemblies. . . . Take away from me the noise of your songs; to the melody of your harps I will not listen. But let justice roll down like waters, and righteousness like an ever-flowing stream. [Amos 5:21, 24–24.]

The Old Testament reminds us again and again that God will not tolerate unbelief and that he is angry with an unbelieving people. But let us beware of being self-righteous! There are plenty who would rush to condemn others. We must be loving and considerate, and not rush at everything with insensitivity, dismissing all and sundry as faithless, unless there is a blank refusal to change. People don't always suddenly get filled with faith overnight; they need to be led and encouraged a step at a time to believe God in practical ways. But many have given in and allowed their unbelief and fear to prevent any forward movement. The church is called to be a pilgrim people, on the move, obeying, living under the direction of Christ. When it loses sight of where it is going, its vision fails and faith is lost. It stagnates and dies, and that which is alive, if it is to survive, is forced to break away and begin something fresh. Those who complain about new churches springing up today usually have only themselves to blame. Let us not be afraid, but hold hands and walk steadily forward together.

Insecurity

Most of us are deeply insecure. Often those who make the most noise and appear to have most confidence are in fact the most insecure. Why is it that many churches today, although they have seen the reality of corporate leadership, will not actually move their church into that form of government? Why is it that many people today understand what it means to have a local body of believers and yet will not allow their church to be involved with others?

The reason very often is deep insecurity, particularly in the leaders. There are many ministers and pastors today who have found their degree of security in life by being recognized as being the pastor, the vicar or, in some cases, the elder. That is why, in talking to these people, we need to be very sensitive and understanding, and realize when we speak about corporate ministry and about unity that we may well be saying something very threatening to those in positions of authority. At the same time many leaders need to face up to their insecurity and recognize that it is often a reason for holding up the work of God.

Clericalism is probably the single greatest problem in the church today. It is entangled with pride, status, fear and insecurity.

What will you do?

When God sees all this in his church, no wonder he weeps for his people. You can almost hear again the words of longing that were spoken in the prophet Isaiah, when God talked about his people as the vineyard. He commented, 'What more could I have done for my vineyard?' What more could God have done for his people? Was the cross not sufficient? Is the gift of the Holy Spirit not sufficient? When the prophet Daniel saw the reason why the people of Israel were in exile, he did not point the finger or condemn others, but he saw the sin that was in himself, and the sin that was in the people, and he began to pray and to repent. And the moment he began to repent, God began to set in motion the deliverance of his people.

Our response to realizing God's feelings for his church will firstly be that we repent. If I see the problem only in others and not in myself then I am blind! But repentance must be worked out in action.

If you have heard from God, then you will do something that demonstrates that you really have heard. What will you do?

5

What are you building?

'What are you actually building?' asked Tony, a close friend for many years, as I finished sharing my busy and varied life of dashing from one Christian event to another. There was a rather embarrassed silence, followed by my trying rather feebly to justify my existence. But it left me thinking. What was I actually building? My own little kingdom? Was I just helping to maintain dead institutions? Was I guilty, in the words of a famous South American pastor, of building a 'pile of bricks rather than a building'?

Our churches today are full of different sorts of people. Some are full of activity. They run this group and that, and sit on all sorts of committees. Every night finds them at some church function or other. They would certainly qualify as 'active members of the church'. They are people who say, 'We are fully involved in our local church.' But what are many of these people actually building? Are they merely allowing an institution to survive, or building a church that will reach the world?

Very often gifted people are tremendously busy in the life of the church, but they don't stop to assess whether their great *activity* is actually related somewhere along the line to *productivity* in the kingdom of God. The only way to be productive is to be obedient. It is possible to confuse and substitute commitment to the church and its activities for commitment to Christ!

Others attend church on Sunday plus a Bible study or prayer meeting during the week, and are totally committed to the church. But although they may be gifted in many areas, actually in reality they do nothing. Usually the biggest churches have the greatest number of inactive people in them. Gifted, talented people sit in the pews week after week and their faith is never stretched, never tested. Rarely are they required to exercise faith at all. Usually, the bigger and more successful the church, the more there is of this sort of tragically wasted manpower. The trouble is that life is very comfortable like this, especially if you have a good job, a family and a nice home. A good undemanding church life in which you 'do' just enough to make you feel involved, just puts the icing on the top of the cake.

So we in fact have a vast sleeping church, building nothing, and being tragically ineffective. The problem is not the size of the church, but its failure to function as a body and to gear itself to real growth. A large church must be sufficiently subdivided to give everybody the opportunity to function. A church covering a large area may divide and form two units, but the division would be, as I have already said, on the basis of geography and not denomination.

If you look at the Pentecostal Church in South America, which is growing so rapidly, you see there a pattern in which every believer is a worker. Their main drive and energy is directed not at their business life or leisure time, but in serving Christ along with the other believers. They grow because their faith is stretched. If British Christians don't grow it may be because they are rarely called upon to exercise faith.

The psalmist said, 'Unless the Lord builds the house, those who build it labour in vain' (127:1). There are many leaders today building very hard, with great enthusiasm and energy, but they are not building what the Lord is building. What are you building? If you are building what God is building, if you are primarily concerned with his kingdom, then you won't be the slightest bit concerned who gets the credit. You won't mind if someone else's work prospers at your expense, in fact you will encourage it if it will further the kingdom. Now that attitude takes a man whose heart is being opened to God's heart. It is very hard. Most, if they are honest, are building their own congregations, their own work, and usually people who build their own work, build it so they can sit on the top of it to be admired. That is why you will see lively, growing churches near one another, apparently competing with each other. Each is evangelizing the same area. Each is praying for the unconverted. But both, while acknowledging the other's existence, are being careful not to co-operate too closely, for fear of losing some people to the other fellowship.

A minor prophet with a major prophecy

Where is it?

I have seen grown men with large hallelujah smiles, carrying enormous black Thompson Chain Reference Bibles, sitting with a look of sheer panic on their faces. I have seen clergy, pretending that they had not brought their Bibles with them. I have seen enthusiastic young people with a look of enormous relief on their faces that they left their gleaming new NIV behind; and all because the preacher says...'Will you turn with me to the book of Haggai.' It's a call that inspires prayer as people fumble through their Bibles conscious of those around them looking on with interest, whispering, 'Just this once Lord, let me find it first time!'

Short but sharp

However difficult it is to find, and although it may be very short, the prophecy of Haggai speaks right into our present situation. It describes a time of restoration. The people were back in Jerusalem. Doubtless their hearts were full of thanksgiving to God for his goodness. They were busy. They were actively building. But nothing seemed really to be going right. Crops failed. Money disappeared as though the bags had holes in them (inflation?). They ate plentifully but they never seemed to be satisfied. They put on clothes but never seemed to get warm.

Why was this? The explanation of the prophet is so simple, some would call it naïve. They were building, but they were building the wrong thing. Their energies were spent on themselves; their houses, their fields, their comforts, their security. And God deliberately frustrated everything they did—because he loved them. He knew that if they were to make a go of it back

57

in the land, it would only be because their lives were centred on him. From the moment they began to build the temple, the place of worship and sacrifice, the place in which God could put his presence, and where he alone would receive glory, they began to find God's hand was with them in all that they did.

Here surely is a question for all of us: 'Is it a time for you to be cosy in your church and in your home, while the house of God lies in ruins?' Consider in reality how we have fared. In our churches, are we really experiencing what you would expect in the 'normal church life' of the early chapters of Acts? In our personal lives, do we see the hand of God in faithful provision for all our needs? I don't mean for a minute that wealth is a sure sign of blessing, but the ability to be satisfied with what you have certainly is. All of us need to meditate on this short book and let God speak to us about it and how it applies to us and to our situation. But we must do so with an open heart, and then it may result in a radical change in our attitude to church life.

What does it mean to 'build the house of the Lord'? Surely it is to build the church. What is the church? It is the body of believers in any one locality. In fact it is more than that. For it covers those not yet converted. Evangelism is involved in building his house. Is that what you are involved in?

The heart to build

Many have found the picture described in the book of Nehemiah particularly helpful. His burden to build came from his broken heart over the city in ruins. As the people built they were building one city, but each working specifically in his own place. Most of the time it would appear that they built nearest to their own home. What a good pattern that is. The meetings in homes with a concern for the immediate locality, but the vision that that is only a part of the whole of the local church.

They built and worked in families. But the secret of Nehemiah's success in the rebuilding work comes again and again in the early chapters: 'The people had a mind to work.' Isn't that our greatest need today—for people who have a mind to build and work? The writer records that, with one family, 'their nobles did not put their necks to the work of the Lord'. How many times could that be repeated today?

Under attack

The first verbal attack the people received was: 'What is this thing you are doing? Are you rebelling against the King?' The accusation was of rebellion. Isn't that the cry today as soon as people begin to take the biblical concept of the church seriously? 'You are rebelling against authority.' What authority? Man-made authority? In some cases, it is true, hurt is being caused by a very definite rebellious spirit that is unwilling to recognize divinely appointed authority in men who are part of the 'established church'. But provided men and women are under authority, isn't it time for a bit more rebellion of the right kind!

Then in chapter 4 come the attacks on the superficiality of their work. 'It'll never last.' 'It's a nine-day wonder.' 'Look at the materials they've got to work with.' I'm sure the Jewish authorities must have said and certainly thought the same things about the motley crowd of folks that followed Jesus around, and the same murmurings were heard in the early days of the church. The book of Nehemiah is rich with illustrations that teach of God's design and pattern for his church, but this isn't the place to take it further. Suffice to say, they succeeded because they had a vision, they had a will to work and the hand of the Lord was upon them. But when you build what God is building, the hand of God is always upon you. The opposition is strong and subtle, but God will fufil his purposes.

Prophetic leadership

They succeeded too because there was a man who was not primarily interested in repairing one or two gates, the ones he liked best; no, his heart was for the whole city. The church in any one locality is only going to be built not only when the people have a heart or a vision for it, but when the leaders have the same vision. In so many cases, leaders have got a hold of this vision but have used it to strengthen their own personal work. 'If there is to be one church in this locality, everybody should come and join us.' It doesn't usually work that way.

Speak to the bones

The prophet Ezekiel was a man who saw a vision which revealed the real state of God's people from God's perspective. God had opened his heart to him, telling him of his deep anger at the behaviour of the shepherds, the leaders. He told Ezekiel how he himself would take matters into his own hands and lead the people back together again. (And today, God will again bypass those leaders who will not go with him.) Then he showed Ezekiel the valley full of bones. He didn't call him to rush down into the valley to do everything he could to stick the bones in the right place next to each other. Ezekiel would have been there for months!

Can you imagine the chaos if Ezekiel got it wrong—a man with odd legs and arms upside down! But he spoke the word, shared the vision, and the bones began to move. God is bringing people together. It needs men to prophesy, speak out the vision of God to every community. He will do the rest.

It's not that organization isn't important, it's just that this work is too big for us to organize! We must co-operate with the Holy Spirit in what he is doing. Then, as we see what God is doing, we will feel the call of God upon us to begin to cry to his Spirit to come and breathe life into the body.

What is there today for God to breathe life into? Scattered bones. If there was a further outpouring of the Spirit of God in Britain today, would we have an army stand up? No, dismembered limbs rushing around furiously! In some places God would be able to move more freely than in others because people have prepared channels for his power to flow.

In different places in Britian today, there are the obvious signs of the coming together of bodies who are committed and working for the same ends. If you look carefully you will not find any greater degree of power in terms of outreach and evangelism. The formation of bodies is only the first step. Unity in itself will not bring about revival. But when there is a body available for

God's use, and the breath of God then begins to blow, then that body becomes an instrument in God's hand. Do you want God to blow with tremendous power through your town or village? Then you will work to respond to God's call to build his church. You will work towards the formation, in your locality, of a body of people who are committed to each other in love.

We must examine how we spend our time. We need to go through our week bit by bit and work out whether the energy, time and money that we are using is actually going towards building the kingdom of God. If the answer is no, then there needs to be a complete reappraisal of what we are doing. With whom are we in relationship; who are we closest to in God's church? Are there those with whom we can build the kingdom of God where we live? It's time we got into relationship with the right people.

6

The body of Christ

Clergy and ministries

One of the biggest areas of bottleneck and confusion with regard to building the local body lies in the whole concept of ministry. It is extremely important to get this right, because effective ministry will release important gifts in the church, and ineffective ministry will prevent them really growing. We have all got to grasp this particular nettle if the church is going to be effective. If we see that God's purpose is to build a body in any given locality, then we have to have some understanding of the nature of the body of Christ. In the midst of this we must also sensitively and yet uncompromisingly face the whole question of professional clergy.

In 1 Corinthians 12 Paul gives three basic principles:

1. Every Christian is a part of the body of Christ universally and locally. No person is more or less important than anyone else. We tend to look at the church and pick out key people as important to its life. Then we see the mass of people as members without any particular function. 'It is really neither here nor there whether they belong or not, although of course it's nice to see them around!' Paul's principle is quite different. If any Christian is not functioning and in relationship, the whole body suffers. We don't actually believe that. We say we do, but we don't. We all wish we were like the hand with all its vitality and life, but the drudgery and monotony of being a foot is really very

unexciting! So let's not bother! No wonder we have a crippled, slow-moving church.

Everyone likes eyes—we comment on each other's eyes. Lovers admire each other's eyes. But whoever complimented his girl-friend on her ears! Who wants to be like that, and not get any credit, or be unseen? So let's not bother. No wonder the church isn't hearing from God! We are led by the exciting go-getting type, full of drive, but those who actually hear from God and bring gentle quiet discernment (and it's often the women) are ignored and therefore opt out. The greatest ministry any of us can have is to encourage other people to find their gifts and help them to use them. We are all so insecure and easily threatened that we find it so hard to do. So we do the opposite and, filled with jealousy, spend our time criticizing and destroying one another.

We suffer not because there aren't enough talented people about, but because the mass of one-talent folk never invest their talent; they hide it. What is your gift? Are you encouraging other people to discover and use theirs?

2. Paul's second basic principle is that all the parts are different. All of us are different. The church's richness lies in fabulous variety, that is the variety of God's creation. We all have different personalities, abilities and gifts. All that is required of us is that we do our part and be ourselves in the fullest sense.

There is always a danger of wanting to conform to a type. What a shame that we tend to get together with people who are like-minded, or who talk and behave like we do, or worship in our way. Why should that be? Why can't we rejoice in our variety instead of allowing it to divide us? If we were to have meetings for the whole body in our locality and people stayed away because it wasn't their style of worship, or their sort of people, what a tragedy that would be! We divide the young in the church from the older people. The old find the young difficult because of all their enthusiasm and life. The young find the old too staid and dull. The youth have vision and energy, and the old have wisdom and experience. What a combination! Yet so rarely are they allowed to combine.

Why can't we be satisfied with our particular gifts? If only I had... if only I was... is the cry of so many hearts. Paul's sense of humour underlines the futility of such thinking. 'If the whole body were an ear...!' It is the same principle with the gifts of the Spirit. They are given to the body. We get so worried about how many gifts people have. Surely the important thing is that all the gifts are present in the body. We are told that they are 'manifestations of the Spirit for the common good'. It doesn't matter at all who uses them, as long as the body has them expressed in its midst. Yet we're so individually orientated in our thinking, and so self-centred, that we can't grasp this simple truth.

3. Lastly, Paul says that we all need each other. That's another simple biological fact of the human body. It's quite obvious if we think about it just for a moment. But how can we ever discover and apply this mutual care and support if we never relate? Leprosy is a disease that results in the extremities, such as fingers and toes, being severely damaged. The reason for it is in the failure of the nerves. The fingers no longer feel pain and so get damaged very easily.

The body of Christ today is very battered because it is unable to feel either the pain or the joy of its members. How *can* we do this if we are not relating?

But what is this body we are talking about? Is it the local Baptist church, or the local Anglican church? No, a thousand times no! That may be a part of it, but it is not the body. The body is the entire community of believers, wherever they may 'go to church'.

I can think of two thriving fellowships very close to each other. It it absolutely clear to the outsider that one has what the other lacks in terms of ministries and vice versa. But up to now they have had tremendous problems relating. *Tragedy* is the only word I can think of to describe such a situation.

Ministries

Should women be ordained into the ministry? This has been a major issue in the Church of England in recent years, but it's

64

really a non-question. Surely the first question should be—'Is the ordained ministry (as we know it), or professional clergy, a biblical concept?' I believe the answer is no. So the question of women in that role cannot be tackled, since men should not be 'in the ministry' either, as we understand ministry today. However, in terms of ministries in the body of Christ, women have a place as well as men.

The biblical pattern (and ultimately you must decide if the Bible is to be the basis of your belief and lifestyle or not) makes it clear that God has put a variety of ministry gifts in the church or local body. He has not put these ministries in one denominational church but in the local body. (So they will not be found until we find the body.) These ministries are primarily to equip the saints—believers—to be effective in their own ministry.

People have called these 'foundational' ministries. Well, foundational ministries should really hardly be seen, because they support the other ministries. If leaders are really being effective with their gifts, then they are allowing everyone else in the body to be effective in their gifts and releasing them into ministry. In other words, theirs are enabling and serving gifts (see Ephesians 4). They are not there to do all the work and take all the glory. They are there to help the other members to function properly. If they do a really good job they will be background workers who go hardly noticed at the end of the day. What a far cry from what we have today!

One-man band

The one-man ministry is still very much in evidence today, even in charismatic circles. Is this biblical? The answer must be no, although we cannot deny the importance of men with strong leadership and pioneering qualities. These are often men with apostolic ability who are pioneers and probably should never become settlers. It is difficult when you have set a fellowship on its feet not to stay around for ever. Some of these people need to be encouraged to move on or be released to travel. The danger is that strong personalities may form a church that can't survive without them—so they are afraid of leaving in case it all collapses.

There is a lot of double-talk about. Many are willing to embrace concepts of renewal that suit them and dismiss others that don't. Many take a strong biblical line on certain aspects of doctrine, but seem to go amazingly silent on issues that affect them personally. How can you have a biblical attitude to the church and maintain a belief in a one-man professional ministry?

Now to say this can cause a lot of people to feel very threatened—which is why it must be said with love and understanding. No wonder so many clergy and pastors are trapped by denominationalism. They are paid by the denomination, therefore in effect they are owned by them. They have in the final analysis to toe the line. If people really believe they have been called by God into the ministry, then why aren't more prepared to stop taking their pay from their denomination and trust God to provide for them? A labourer is certainly worthy of his hire, but who should be hiring him! Surely the money should come through the local believers.

Most people find themselves in a one-man situation because when God called them into full-time ministry the place into which they were called was already a one-man situation. But it doesn't have to stay that way. God has put you there in order to change the situation, not to be conformed by it. Clergy have to learn to become members of their own fellowship and elders in the local body, as well as teaching their congregation to become ministers! How will this ever be, unless a few people have the courage to break the system!

Now here's the terrible problem. 'If I do that,' says someone, 'I may be left with nothing. All I have known is the ministry. It's my status and my security. I am somebody, I am the vicar, the pastor. Now you are putting all that at risk.' Well, yes and no. Lay people must encourage the clergy to find their ministry in the church. Clergy must see themselves as a ministry, possibly an elder of the local body. Maybe they have pastoral responsibilities for one congregation in their local body. After all, these ministry gifts are not usually contained in congregations but in the whole local body. The eldership of the local body may consist of some 'clergy' and some 'lay people', although of course both these terms are unbiblical. The distinction between clergy and lay must eventually be removed because it doesn't actually exist!

It is easy for house-church people to be insensitive here. Usually in their situation they have fellowships full of committed people who 'tithe' and therefore there is no difficulty in providing for the full-time worker. In a hard inner-city Anglican church where the minister is already financially desperate it is no easy thing to look to the Lord for finance. So let's be sensitive. Don't be critical, be generous. The wealthy fellowships should be paying out to support these harder works. Having said all this, it needs to be stressed that although a one-man, jack-of-all-trades ministry is wrong, God does often give gifts of *leadership* to one or two people. It is very important to distinguish between these two concepts—on the one hand someone who 'does it all', and on the other hand someone who leads and serves all, encouraging each member of the body to find his or her ministry. I would certainly not want to encourage the squashing of the leadership and pioneering gifts that God has given to his church.

Too many Revs!

If only the term 'Reverend' could be dropped! What is the justification for it? Surely only the Lord can be called reverend! Yes, there are reasons, but usually they are a means of disguising the real issue which is at stake, namely status. So many people believe this in theory, but where is it in practice?

Consider the words of Jesus:

Everything they do is done for men to see: They make their phylacteries wide and the tassels of their prayer shawls long; they love the place of honour at banquets and the most important seats in the synagogues; they love to be greeted in the market places and to have men call them 'Rabbi'.

But you are not to be called 'Rabbi', for you have only one Master and you are all brothers. And do not call anyone on earth 'father', for you have one father, and he is in heaven. Nor are you to be called 'teacher', for you have one Teacher, the Christ. The greatest among you will be your servant. For whoever exalts himself will be humbled, and whoever humbles himself will be exalted. [Mt 23:5–12 NIV.]

I don't think it could be much clearer.

Let's remember that the Lord wants a body: 'He has no hands but our hands to do his work today; he has no feet but our feet to lead men in his way. He has no voice but our voice to tell men how he died; he has no help but our help to lead them to his side.'

Shepherding

We have seen over the past years two opposite extremes concerning the whole area of pastoral care. It is clear from Scripture that God has put pastors in the church (the word 'pastor' being equally well translated 'shepherd'). We are all aware that in a very real sense 'the Lord is our shepherd' and it is to him that we should look, listen and follow. But God has put in his church those who will be human agents in the exercise of pastoral care.

Let's look at the two extremes.

Slackness

In most cases, because the minister is so overworked, pastoral care is almost totally neglected or confined to those in particular need. Most of us have a natural aversion to being corrected and have strong independent spirits, so that we shy away from anyone who wants to get too close. And so we miss out on the encouragement, protection and help that pastoral care can provide. All of us need pastoral care and would benefit from putting ourselves in someone else's hands. And that means not just when we feel like it.

But in a one-man ministry how can anybody pastor a church and provide the personal care that every individual needs? No wonder the majority of people never have any such care and protection. And what of the pastors and leaders? They too need to have a person or people to whom they can look for support, advice and correction, although there is no reason why that has to become a rigid arrangement whereby a man is obligated to do what he is told by someone else. One of the great problems today is that so many ministers are discouraged and disheartened, mainly because nobody has been able to come and give them the pastoral care and advice that they themselves need. They pass out advice to other people but long for somebody to come and give them the same sort of care.

Suffocation

Where the principles of shepherding have been rediscovered, the danger has been suffocation. In some cases it has got to the state where a man or a woman cannot even go shopping without the pastor's consent! Tragically, these sorts of incidences are by no means few and far between. This has several extremely negative effects.

First, it puts power into the hands of people who have no right at all to exercise such influence over another person's life, especially as they are often young and inexperienced themselves. Secondly, it deprives a person of the responsibility of making decisions, which is always destructive and will have very serious consequences for that individual in every aspect of his life. People must always learn to take decisions for themselves, albeit with help and advice from others. Thirdly, it suffocates faith. If someone continually lives under the umbrella of somebody else's faith, then he himself will never exercise personal faith and therefore never grow. When his 'shepherd' is taken away from him, he finds himself very vulnerable because he has never learned to trust the Lord for himself. The wise pastor is a man who lets his sheep have freedom to learn by doing and experiencing, but is always there to protect and to care for them, and to prevent them from coming to harm.

If you rigidly insist that every man is under someone higher up the scale, how ever do you avoid producing a pope? Then you put great power into the hands of a few and you have a very dangerous situation. Under whose authority were Paul or Peter? Surely they were mutually submitted one to the other, which is a good and healthy situation.

Another danger is that you look for oversight from people of your own way of thinking. Today men in the house-churches need to be looking to those still in denominations for mutual support, and vice versa. That would provide a far healthier protection against extremism. Why is it that a church in one part of the country has to look for a man hundreds of miles away for oversight? Are there really not the people nearer to hand? Or is it that there is nobody who will say the right things that they want to hear? One of the negative aspects of any new wave of church leadership will be a tendency towards arrogance among its leaders. A little humility to allow others to have some authority over their lives would certainly reap great rewards—and that includes those who are still part of 'the establishment' but who are obviously men of God, often with far more experience in spiritual matters.

We would do well to remember that in a world full of insecurity, there is a tendency for men and women to look to strong authoritarian structures. In Britain we are becoming more and more open to the possibility of a totalitarian government. It isn't just that it would be implemented from above. It will in fact, even if unconsciously, be gladly received from below. We are creating an environment for ourselves where we will readily accept this type of authority and form of government. We want strong leadership that will tell us what to do, and we are in fact prepared to pay the price provided we are materially stable.

Because we Christians are people of our age and our generation, we are susceptible to strong authoritarian structures coming into the church, which allow us a degree of freedom and yet provide us with great security. But as soon as the church allows this to happen, it is in a strangle-hold, and will consist of vast numbers of people who are ripe for manipulation.

One united church under one human authority is more a picture of antichrist, not of the bride of Christ. Local autonomy is vitally important if we are to maintain freedom. We are not seeking one worldwide monolithic church. That may well happen as the dead structures try and unite at an institutional level, but that is quite a different thing from the unity that there is in the diversity of the bride of Christ. The biblical pattern is not for there to be 'one church' but for a vast number of churches clearly independent in leadership and yet linked in Spirit—each being a part of that 'body of Christ' that is the church of the past, present and future, wholly united under the headship of Christ.

7

New structures for old

So what is the way forward? Up to this point a great deal of what has been said may appear negative. Unless we all face up to the sin in our lives and in the church, we will never be able to discover God's forgiveness and deliverance.

At the same time we must be aware of the pitfalls ahead. If we are not open to the fact that the same problems that have produced death in the old forms are contained potentially in all of us, then we are heading for trouble. The man who points the finger at the Anglican Church, for example, and yet cannot see that in his own idealism he is capable of producing the same animal under another name, is in a dangerous position. Those that see sin in one part of the body that they don't also identify in themselves, have failed to grapple with the real issues. The Israelites that went into the promised land were not a superior breed to those that spent forty years in the wilderness, but they were obedient and responded to God's call to go forward through faith in his word.

It's always easy for those in the honeymoon period of a work to point the finger at those whose work has been going longer and appears to be stuck. It's easy to criticize the elderly elders of a Brethren assembly and to be excited with the young enthusiastic leadership in the new house church, forgetting that those elderly men were enthusiastic pioneers once. It is true they shouldn't have allowed themselves to get stuck, but the warning is there for the younger generation. By all means let's go forward, but let us do so with our eyes open.

The situation we are now faced with in the vast majority of places is that large numbers of people have experienced personal renewal and encouragement in the last few years, and many have also come to Christ. Most of these have stayed faithfully in the denominational churches they were already linked to. They have seen, to a greater or lesser degree, some change in the situation. But if the leadership is rigid, in the end very little happens. If the leaders are alive but the people are rigid, again little changes. So there are a large number of frustrated people longing to see something more happen, deeply concerned to reach the world outside, who are kept alive either by praise rallies, conferences or, if they are fortunate, by a regular home group. Most of these are aware that if their neighbours became Christians, they wouldn't really know what to do with them.

The question many ask is whether everybody should come out of their denominational churches and form new churches in each locality. It is impossible to give one answer to that question because each place requires a different answer. But we can look at the basic principles.

First, the Lord is concerned to reach the world, so what we build in each place must be primarily constructed with that in mind. In other words the structure is to provide for growth in quantity and quality as fast and easily as possible, and it is to allow the principles of body life to be expressed most fully.

Secondly, we must keep in mind the Lord's desire to have a united body of believers in each locality—realizing that it will never be complete as not all Christians will have this vision. This may or may not need a new structure. If there is a Bible-believing, Spirit-led church already in existence that is prepared to become the basis of this body, that's marvellous. We mustn't be frustrated just because it's imperfect. For such a church to become the basis of 'the body', it will have to break free of denominational boundaries—in actuality, if not in name. If not, there will have to be new structures, but these must be built as flexibly as possible, and not be exclusive or separatist, so that they can respond to what God is doing.

The best pattern for real growth to take place is at three levels.

1. The small group (cell)

It has been amazing to find how many towns and villages, during the period of Lent, experimented with inter-denominational house-groups. Almost without exception they created tremendous excitement, and for most it was very sad that at Easter they had to come to a stop. In reality, what was happening was that the body of Christ in that town or village was at last discovering itself, not allowing their differences to separate them, but actually being enriched by each other. What a shame it had to finish! If it happens each Lent period in your area, why don't you just keep going?

But it would be fatal for these groups just to remain as ecumenical ones. They need to become in reality the local expression of the church and not seen as an extra-church activity.

All over the country there is a tremendous growth in home groups. This is one of the new things that God is doing. In fact it's not only true of Britain, but right across the world. God is building his church in home groups! This must be one of the keys to the church's effectiveness in the 1980s and this must be encouraged everywhere and as fast as possible. The main reason for caution in most places, particularly in an interdenominational context, is fear by ministers that they will lose control. But that may not necessarily be a bad thing!

The greatest danger that some people see is that of false teachers devouring the flock, but if we are becoming aware of ministries within the local body, this can be controlled.

In his book *New Wineskins* (Marshall, Morgan & Scott 1977) Howard Snyder concludes the following:

> A small group of 8 or 12 people meeting together informally in homes, is the most effective structure for the communication of the gospel in modern secular urban society. Such groups are better suited to the mission of the Church in today's urban world, than are traditional Church services, institutional Church programmes or the mass communication media. Methodologically speaking, the small group

offers the best hope for the discovery and use of spiritual gifts and renewal within the Church.

He gives eight advantages of small group structure:

1. It is flexible (procedures and functions can change easily).
2. It is mobile (can meet anywhere).
3. It is inclusive (everybody can get involved).
4. It is personal (communication is at a personal level).
5. It can grow by division (endless possibilities of growth).
6. It can be an effective means of evangelism.
7. It requires a minimum of professional leadership.
8. It is adaptable to the institutional church (does not require complete rejection).

He goes on to make this very important conclusion:

> It is questionable whether the institutional Church can have a significant evangelistic ministry today through traditional methods. It may be able to build a denomination and carry out programmes, but it will never be able to turn the world the right side up. If the contemporary Church would shake loose from plant and programmes, from institutionalism and inflexibility, and would return to the dynamic of the early Church, it must seriously and self-consciously build its ministry around the small group as the basic structure.

It is obviously vitally important that the purpose of small groups is defined. The formation of groups is not the end of the story. If they don't have a purpose, a direction, a motivation, they will quickly dwindle and become purely introverted and ineffective. The Christian life is a life of change. The small group is the place that enables us to experience this change.

The group needs to function in a fourfold way.

(a) Godward

They need to be based on worship and prayer so that the focus is on God first. This then creates a desire to hear from God, both through spiritual gifts and the study of the Bible. The Bible study needs always to be applied or it becomes formal and academic.

(b) Saintward

The group provides an ideal opportunity for sharing and caring at a personal level. It can be a place of encouragement, healing and growth, as well as a place of loving correction. A group that determines to 'speak the truth in love' may be initially threatening, but will become incredibly strengthening, and ultimately bring great security. In this regard, the possibilities for group activity are very varied, from Bible study to barbeques! They don't have to be intensely spiritual times. The purpose is to enable the group to get to know one another and to be able to share openly and deeply with one another, as well as to share their lives together.

(c) Worldward

This dimension is vitally important if the full value of small groups is to be realized. If they are geographically based it will be much easier to have both a united concern for those living nearby and also an awareness of the physical (as well as spiritual) needs. In this way, practical acts of kindness can be expressed as a way of sharing Christ's love for those around us. The Christians should be the first to support those in need, whatever that need is. If I belong to a prayer group some miles from my home, there is no way I can pray with real faith and conviction or any sense of feeling for the people in that street or neighbourhood. It is an unreal situation. The group that does not expect to see people converted, and see the group grow and divide, is eventually going to die. This united outward vision will strengthen the group in itself.

Ron Trudinger has this to say in his book *Cells for Life* (Olive Tree Publications 1979):

> Such a group does not exist for itself, it is a proclamation to the wider community around it, the neighbours if you like, of God's excellencies, His character, His attributes. It is a lighthouse in a stormy sea. Or, to use another figure, it is an oasis in a desolate wilderness. A lighthouse glows, but it does not have to organise a campaign. An oasis beckons by just being there. The greenness and water attract the thirsty desert traveller.

So the home cell group whose life is displaying the attributes of

God, does not necessarily have to strain to witness or invite others. Such a group has a magnetism all of its own, and through such the Lord can add to the Church daily such as would be saved. We are beginning to realise that the effective living of these small groups of people in their natural local neighbourhoods is one of God's principal means of evangelism in this day and age.

All around us, at least in the western world, we see decay and deterioration in society's foundations. Broken marriages, couples living together unmarried, broken homes, delinquent children, drug addiction, suicide and increasing crime. When people in these situations see the wholeness, peace, purity and zest of a group of ordinary people relating together with what is to the world abnormal enjoyment and love, there is often a wistful longing to know how this comes about, and who brought it about.

May I add another point that he puts at the end of this statement:

> Surely in these days, God's dream is many thousands of restoration churches around the globe, made up of myriads of cells, small koinonia, Holy Spirit-filled groups of Jesus-love-knit-together people, living as God's society, His alternative society in the world. This is God's now strategy for evangelism.

If you and I want to be part of God's strategy for evangelism, we will be in a local home group made up of Christians in our locality.

If we are to be concerned with our world then intercession will be a vital part of our meeting together. We will need to pray and call upon God to reach out to those around us. Intercession is the work of those who will 'go between'; those who will lay hold of God particularly on behalf of those who don't know him. Intercession often involves real commitment and hard work, and it is often in the place of the small group that we can best intercede.

(d) Satanward

All of us live in a battlefield. It is a battle, Paul reminds us, not against people, flesh and blood, but against Satan. In the past, Satan has been able to prevent believers from being effective by isolating them and then attacking them. But in the context of a group there is a facility for us to pray against the powers of darkness as they attack us individually. There is also the possibility of being able to agree together in effective warfare against his strongholds in the area in which we live, and his work in the lives of those around us. After all, evangelism is warfare. It involves men and women being released from the powers of darkness and brought into the kingdom of God.

2. The large group (congregation)

It must be underlined that the place of growth will be in the cell groups and not in the large group. If we lose sight of that, we will get back to the church being a place you go to on Sundays. We must build such that it would be possible for the church to go on as usual if the large gatherings had to be stopped!

Cell life on its own is inadequate, however, because it fails to provide for the full expression of gifts and ministries in the body. The large group provides for these as well as being a place of corporate worship, teaching and encouragement. The large group is what is usually called a congregation and traditionally meets weekly. It has its own administrative structure and is led by a group of elders, but allows all the members to discover and use their gifts.

3. Celebration

The celebration provides for the whole church in a large town or city to come together on regular occasions to celebrate their oneness and express their unity as a family. The whole church thus worships the Lord together and hears what he has to say to it.

The reason for coming together needs to be like the feast days of the Old Testament, to worship and give thanks to the Lord, and not because a celebrated speaker has come to town! The celebrations of the past have tended to lose direction because they have just been gatherings of individuals, whereas they really need to be gatherings of whole congregations. This can only happen if the leaders relate together, share a common vision, and are prepared to support and encourage each other.

8

Rise up and build

As we set out to build, it is in the belief that God has already prepared the foundations. These foundations are not structures but people. They are Christians who have known the work of the Spirit in their lives and whose desire is to be together with other Christians regardless of background or tradition. The shape of the building is determined by the style of the foundations. The incentive to build will come because we long to see Christians meeting together and not as parts of a fragmented church. It will be spurred on as we have a deep yearning to see the millions outside of the church find a living relationship with Christ and an experience of being part of the family.

The vision before us is that God wants in every locality a body of believers through whom he can reach the world and in whom he can show his glory. Our calling is to be labourers with him in bringing these people together into a fellowship of Christians. We are to see to it that the company of believers is subdivided into small groups who love and care for each other and who reach out to those around them. This may end up by being a reformed denomination or a completely new expression of church life. It could be either. Our aim should not be to build the perfect church, because it will always be made up of imperfect people. But it is the Lord's desire to have 'a people for his own possession' and the world is waiting to see it. The call on each of us is to 'rise up and build', to be a part of the new thing God is doing and for which he has been preparing us.

When Ezekiel began to prophesy, he heard a rattling noise

caused by the movement of bones. Today, as God builds his church, there will be a movement of people. It won't be a rushing around in frantic activity, but simply a movement of people finding each other. If we are to be the people of God in this generation who will bring Christ to this country and stand up an exceeding great army, then we must obey the voice of the Lord.

We must 'hear the word of the Lord' both individually and corporately by listening carefully to what God is saying. What I'm outlining here are only intended to be principles. Every situation is different and demands that together we seek God for his way ahead. We can learn from others, but we must not be pressurized into a uniformity that demands we copy everyone else. These principles demand that we shake off man-made tradition or we'll never move forward.

There are certain basic questions that have to be asked in any building programme, so let's look at those now.

Why are you building?

The purpose of building will define the structure and layout of what you build. If you want a house, you don't build a bridge. The purpose needs to be kept clearly in view at all times and never allowed to fade. We must build at this time with two objectives.

First, we are building for God, that is a people who long to fulfil his desire for unity among his children, through whom he can express his glory and power, and in whom he is clearly seen to be Lord. He is wanting above all 'a people of praise'.

Secondly, if we are building for God, we must build at all times with the world in mind. God's desire is a people who will reach the lost. Any other sort of building is a 'folly'. If we know that we are constructing something that is to be the most effective instrument in reaching the unconverted, it will determine how we build. As we build with this clearly in mind, the Lord will start adding to us those who are being saved.

Where are you building?

(a) Evaluate

Every individual needs to evaluate his own situation. It will be difficult if you are comfortable where you are. Every one of us needs to ask the Lord, 'To which body do I belong?' Not 'like to belong' but 'belong'. The likelihood is that it will be where you live. If God has put you in a certain place, then the rest of the body is around somewhere, however small or large, and you need to find it. It may mean severing old links and making new ones. It may mean a traumatic change, breaking away from a comfortable unchallenging situation to step out into the unknown.

If you are already 'in place' you may need to evaluate your function and role within the church.

There are still many places in Britain, particularly new housing areas, where there is no church, and it requires people from outside to come in and begin a new work. In the majority of places, though, it is not a question of *church planting* but of taking what is already there and restructuring that into something that is a more adaptable unit. That is why we need to be careful of those who just want to rush around founding new works alongside an already existing one, without any sensitivity to what is already going on.

(b) Define

You must also define the area in which you feel called to build. It will be an area that is local and realistic, so that you can have real faith for something to happen. The next step is to see who else is building in the area—what already exists. Spy out the land. Build *with* those who also have a heart to build in that place, not independently of them.

With what are you going to build?

Nehemiah began with what he had. He didn't discard it, but he sorted out the rubble from that which could be used. In most places there will be something to start with. Most likely it will be fragmented and broken down, but there are at least stones (living ones!) even if they are not yet in proper relationship. Some will have rolled a long way, but they'll be coming back! Others will be hidden and need to be uncovered. But the key is to start with what you have. Take a good look around. The important thing is to bring together the believers in the area on the basis of the body, not denomination.

How are you going to build?

Every construction needs a plan. Every situation will be different, but mercifully it is 'the Lord who builds the house'. We will need to get from him step by step what we are to do. This means that those who have a vision for this must meet regularly and often together to pray. Nothing of value will be achieved except through prayer. This must be the starting place if we truly believe God is wanting to bring this new thing about.

Leader of leaders

There is a need in every place to have a person or group of people who have a vision not for 'their church' but for 'the area'. They are the ones who need to get all the local Christians together to share the vision. They need to be local people, as they understand the local situation and will be sensitive to it, not wanting to fragment the body any more but whose prime desire is to bring people together. But of course it may well be that advice from folk outside who can bring a degree of objectivity and guidance will be required, in the way that Paul and others did in the early church.

Those that take a lead should be careful to involve and inform existing leaders in the locality. Nothing need be done in a corner secretly. Every opportunity needs to be given for involvement of already existing leadership, provided they are spiritual men. A new local leadership may well emerge that will be a mixture of 'lay people' and 'clergy' in which the lay people are accepted on equal terms with clergy. We must be freed from the old system of clergy dominance. The question is not a matter of clergy or lay, but of realizing to whom God has given the right of leadership in each place. Often outside help is needed in this. It was Paul who appointed the elders in many churches, because he could recognize men of God's calling in each situation.

Principles of structure

(1) INDIVIDUAL

The building will be made up of believers who have a heart to build. It will be those who have freed themselves from denominationalism, even though they may still be in a denomination. Their desire will be to become a part of the body of believers in the area.

Many already have been discouraged but will want to be a part of God's plan for the neighbourhood. The first step, then, is to get as wide a group of Christians from the area together on a number of occasions to worship and pray together and share the vision.

(2) CELL

The next essential step is that every believer should be encouraged to be a committed member of a cell or fellowship group. These will be made up of Christians who are approximately in the same area, although sensitivity is needed in making up the groups.

Many cell groups may already exist. The groups could be of all denominational backgrounds if these are the people who live near each other. If you are not part of such a group, see if one already exists. If not, stretch out your hands to those nearby and get them together. In many places groups already exist, but these need to be drawn together so that they realize they are part of something wider.

The leaders of groups should have responsibility for pastoring those in their group. Therefore leadership training is going to be of vital importance.

The cell group *must* be made up of those who are both committed to Christ and to the people in the group. As a general rule, it is not the place for outsiders, as this may prevent the group developing. Those coming to Christ need both personal help and special groups before they are ready to be part of a cell. When the congregation meets it will be open to a wider group of people. That's why the heart of the local church, which is the sum of the cell groups, is not reflected in the size of the larger meeting.

(3) CONGREGATION

Cell groups by themselves are only part of the life of a local church. There must be a degree of structure and discipline, and also opportunity for corporate expression. How can this be?

(a) The leaders of cell groups need to be meeting regularly so that there is a common sense of direction, opportunity for sharing needs and praying together.

(b) The people need to be meeting on a regular basis, something more than an occasional celebration. They need to experience regular congregational life together.

When will you build?

The time to build is *now*, because the foundations have been laid. Of course in many places in the country this has been going on for some time, and there are tremendously exciting examples of new churches forming from scratch and new churches coming from old structures.

In order for there to be minimum tearing and hurt in the local area, and to give opportunity for as many as possible to be involved, many feel it wisest for new fellowships to meet at a time that does not clash with already existing services. (This may initially be just the coming together of cell groups.) There is nothing holy about 11.00 and 6.30 on Sundays! There is no reason why new fellowships shouldn't meet on a Friday or Saturday night or even Sunday afternoons—whichever is more convenient. This may or may not be a temporary measure, but it gives people time to see what is going on, to decide where they want to put their energy. It also means many can belong to the new thing and attend the old in order to be a blessing to the people there. Always remember that God may have given up on the institution but he has not given up on his people, and he's longing to reach out to them and bless them. Although we can be free to go, we must be sure that our commitment is to the new work.

What will you build?

If we begin by drawing together believers in an area, encouraging them to meet in home groups and bringing them together on a regular basis, certain things are likely to happen:

(1) In an area where there is no living congregation, a new congregation will form, even if it begins small in a home or school. It will not be in competition with any other congregation because there was nothing there before. It will grow by people coming to Christ in the area and joining this local body. This is an exciting possibility in many places, and we could see a lot of new churches over the next few years. Let's hope this will *not* mean lots of new buildings as well—they so easily become idols and monuments.

(2) An already existing congregation will be flexible enough to be the congregation that expresses the body of Christ locally. If it is to do this fully, it must be free of denominational restrictions and be released from a clergy-dominated leadership. There must be a desire to be as flexible as possible, to discover patterns of leadership and growth that are based on body principles. This situation is already emerging, but in many cases the denominational hold prevents people from going all the way. In fact, in many cases where this is true, it is the leadership rather than the people who will not be freed from their denominationalism. This is particularly true in Anglican churches that are apparently renewed but where the clergy are Anglican at heart. Sadly it means that a fellowship stops short of all that God has in store for it.

(3) Two or more local congregations will come together to be one united expression of the church. Even if there are physically too many people to meet in one place, they will none the less be united in heart and vision. This will involve sacrifice, but the rewards will be great.

(4) In a place where there are many denominational units which have experienced a certain amount of renewal, but which are resisting the call to move forward, a new expression of

congregational life will have to form, even if it does not initially meet on a Sunday. There will be a new eldership to whom people will look for leadership. This is abhorrent to some and termed divisive, but it is going to be absolutely vital in very many places if anything of lasting value is going to be achieved. To bring some of the fragments together in an already fragmented church is not divisive but in fact healing. If there is no existing congregation willing to respond to become that local expression of the body of Christ, then a new congregation will have to be formed—even if it is not a Sunday congregation. I believe that this will be the case and indeed should be so in many, many places.

The time has come to stop propping up dying institutions and sapping the energy of believers while the world outside is crying out for Christ. There is an inbuilt attitude, very common among us, that says 'at all costs support the system'. *It's time we took our eyes off the system and remembered the world.* The key to this is that any new fellowship must have service as its prime goal. That means to serve the community as well as the rest of the Christian church in that area. It must not be separatist and exist for itself, but become an agent of healing and not of hurt, looking always to serve the wider community rather than protecting its own interests.

In all these situations, the new work will fall apart if it is not founded on the cell group principles described earlier.

Divisive issues

There are three major aspects of church life that are going to be areas of debate.

Holy communion

Part of the old system dictates that it is the prerogative of the clergy to officiate at communion, the celebration of the Lord's supper. Without in any way minimizing the importance of communion or the reverence with which we should treat it, it's time we were freed from this attitude which is really a part of the old power structure of the clergy.

Although we can participate in small groups, it is probably most appropriate when the whole church is assembled, as it enables us to remember our unity brought through Christ's death and resurrection.

Baptism

Or 'ssh, you know what!' Baptism is a subject that nobody really wants to talk about, as it is apparently so controversial. Yet it is quite clear in Scripture that repentance, baptism in water and baptism in the Spirit are a part of the 'one baptism' or initiation into the Christian life. We do people a terrible disservice if we deny them the opportunity to be baptized. We in Britain now live in a mission situation, and if we are to be involved in bringing people from a heathen background to Christ we *must* encourage baptism. Some who have been baptized as infants may well decide that that is their baptism in God's sight. That is between them and the Lord. But for a large number of people that will not be the case, and they must have the opportunity to be baptized. We must not keep silent on this issue.

Worship

Many are afraid that being part of a new type of church life will mean endless chorus singing and clapping. I don't see why this should be so. I believe that there has been a reaction against liturgy that has produced this common picture of charismatic worship. Let's pray that in these new situations we will have the openness to embrace forms and patterns of worship old and new in the freedom of the Spirit. We must not discard the liturgy and music of the past because it became fossilized by tradition, but benefit from what is good in it. Our worship needs to be relevant, full of variety and life.

And they said, 'Let us rise up and build.'

9

Power from above

Another Pentecost! Isn't that the great need today in the church? Not merely personal renewal, but corporate revival. If you could sum up the desire you have for your fellowship. wouldn't it be summed up in those two words? Another Pentecost!

But what is the secret of such an outpouring? And how can it be maintained? It lies in unity—not ecclesiastical unity, but a living unity that is expressed in our daily lives.

Pentecost

'They were all with one accord in one place' (Acts 2:1 AV). It is often taught that one of the results of Pentecost was to bring unity among believers. We are told that the Holy Spirit gives unity. But the unity of the early church existed in measure before the outpouring of the Spirit. It was to a united group of believers that the Holy Spirit came. We are not called to wait for the Holy Spirit to bring unity. We must work for unity. Our responsibility is to come together. We can do something about it. And then he will come! The glory of the Lord filled the tabernacle when it was built. The glory of the Lord filled the temple when it was built. Let's build his church, that his glory might fill his people.

Oil on the beard

'Behold how good and pleasant it is when brothers dwell in unity!... For there the Lord has commanded the blessing, life for evermore' (Ps 133:1, 3). Blessing already commanded! Blessing is defined in this psalm as:

1. Oil on the beard of Aaron

In other words, the anointing of the Spirit on the priesthood. And the priesthood in the New Testament is the priesthood of every believer. What is that?

EVANGELISM

First it is the ministry of bringing God to man and man to God. The priest was the 'bridge-builder'. How can that work ever be effective without the Holy Spirit? That question is clearly answered by all our schemes, plans, campaigns and meetings that show so little fruit. Today many people are talking about evangelism, but very little evangelism is really happening. Even those evangelists who are busy would accept that they are only scratching the surface. We need the power of the Spirit.

WORSHIP

Secondly there is the ministry of bringing the sacrifice of praise to the Lord. How can *that* be effective without the Holy Spirit? Look at the barrenness and dryness of so much of what passes for worship. Where is the spontaneity and the joy of men and women in love with their Lord? In most cases it has become nothing more than a weekly ritual, or should we call it 'rutual'?

We are called to be witnesses. We are called to worship. But if they are to be valid at all, there must be an anointing of God upon them: the anointing that God has promised and is longing to give. Where does the anointing for witness and worship come from? It comes from the Holy Spirit. He has promised to come to the place where people dwell in unity.

2. Water on Mount Hermon

Our second picture of blessing is the fragrance of fruitfulness. The fruit of the Spirit is love, joy, peace and so on. They cannot be attained by striving or by trying, for they are fruit. How can a man or a community show forth those supernatural elements without the Holy Spirit? Where is this unusual love and joy experienced and expressed? It comes in the place of unity. Not because of unity as an end in itself, but because the Holy Spirit comes where he sees unity.

Dwelling not meeting

The expression of unity into which God commanded an out-pouring was not a coming together that was merely occasional and exceptional, as in times of celebration, however valuable that might be. Those are an expression of spiritual unity, but not of functional or experiential unity. The unity that God is looking for is a unity that is functional, and the only way for that to happen is for it to be expressed where we live or dwell. That can then be a day-by-day expression of real oneness that does not have to be denied on certain days because our commitments are to different local organizations.

The oneness we express on Saturday at the celebration is denied again on Sunday and throughout the week by our separation into groups with different names. Where we discover unity of spirit but are members of different denominational clubs, we are not dwelling in unity. Dwelling in unity means living in unity. In other words I am united with the Christians with whom I live, and there is nothing that divides us. We are committed to the same task, the same vision, the same Lord. 'By this all men will know that you are my disciples, if you have love for one another.' This can most effectively be seen at street-level.

Dem dry bones

'Breathe upon these slain, that they may live' (Ezek 37:9). Into what did the breath of life come? Was it to a mass of individual limbs lying strewn across the valley? What would have happened if life had come into them? What a sight! It certainly would not have constituted an 'exceeding great army'; it would have been an exceeding great mess. First of all the bones came together to form a lot of united bodies. Of themselves they were lifeless. That is true of unity. The united body of believers is as powerful or powerless as a mass of individuals who are disunited, but when the Spirit blows through a body the effect is far, far greater than when he blows through isolated individuals.

We pray today for revival. But God in his wisdom and goodness waits for the body of Christ to begin to come together, so that he can move through that and its effectiveness is far greater. If we do not get to grips with this now, we will never do it in times of revival. Then the blessing could be lost as fast as it is gained. 'Come together in Jesus' name' as the Holy Spirit begins to move with power, for God will then have instruments that he can use, not just a few dedicated preachers.

Self-worship

Beware of self-worship. There is a danger of building so that people glory in the church. They look at it, admire it, and the body itself becomes the centre of attention. The body is there to bring attention to the head. Jesus is the head of the body. The more efficient and balanced the body, the greater the freedom that is given to the head to work and express himself. The more effective the church, the less it is noticed, as the people become more and more taken up with Jesus. Otherwise, you become like the man who decided to take exercise to keep fit, and ended up training hard for people to admire his physique. The church will never have a wonderful physique, to be admired, but it does need to be fit!

Breathe on us, breath of God

'You are supposed to have shared leadership—we have that. You should have all denominations together—we have that. You're meant to have house-groups—we've got them. In fact, we seem to have it all, but we don't seem to be any more effective.' The words of a friend to me recently, describing his church fellowship on a new housing estate.

It goes to show that there is no formula to blessing. It does not come because we have done everything right, or it would be the product of man's initiative and ability. Blessing only comes by a sovereign work of the Holy Spirit. The united bodies in Ezekiel's vision, although functionally perfect, were no more able to do anything than the pile of dry bones. But when the breath came, the effectiveness was terrific.

We now need to be crying to God to pour out his Spirit upon the church and the area in which we live. We need to 'prophesy to the wind'. It is time to call upon God for revival power, to open the floodgates and to send rain on the thirsty ground. If he seems slow in coming it isn't his lack of willingness, but his desire to come where he is really wanted.

If we ever believe we can be effective purely through having right structures and methods, we are dead. Our only hope is in the Holy Spirit. Today the characteristic of church prayer meetings must be a united cry for the Holy Spirit to come in power. The reason so many prayer meetings are poorly attended is that we have lost sight of our need. If we only knew what he could do, we'd pray until the power of God came among us. But there is a rising tide of prayer in Britain today, and that is why as you look round there are signs of spring, as new life is again appearing in the church.

10

Into battle

So we come together to build. We wait on the Holy Spirit. We mean business, and we determine to put all our energy into building a renewed and restored church so that revival can come to this land.

And the enemy doesn't like it.

We have some disturbing truths to face before we can even think of becoming an effective witness to the power of God in this land. For it is vital that we first of all have an understanding of the conflict that we are certain to be engaged in. There is opposition to God's work and we need to be prepared for the battle—and assured of the victory.

So before we take a closer look at the principles that should underlie the church's corporate witness, we must first draw up a battle plan and consider our strategy against the true enemy of God's people.

> Soldiers of Christ arise, and put your armour on,
> Strong in the strength which God supplies
> Through his eternal Son.
> From strength to strength go on,
> Wrestle and fight and pray,
> Tread all the paths of darkness down
> And win the well-fought day.

Almost twenty years ago a bunch of raw recruits made history as they pounded up and down an army parade ground in their heavy drill boots. They signalled the end of an era. With every thumping step that echoed across the barracks square, the making and breaking of a generation of British youth drew nearer. Since that last group of recruits passed out in December 1962, a whole generation has grown up free from the duty of national service. They are no longer required to sign up for Queen and country for two years of their life—unless of course they want to. In fact, before the Falklands dispute with Argentina, more than a generation had elapsed without the threat of war. The result was that the 'fighter mentality' lessened with the passing years.

This is precisely what has happened in the church too. We are failing to recognize that we are actually engaged in a battle. But it is not a physical battle, it is spiritual warfare. It is so easy to think of the Christian life as a playground with swings and roundabouts. A joyride. We miss the point that when we become Christians we are joining an *army*. It is an army already engaged in conflict.

The Lord is sending out a call in these days to his people. It is a call to battle. When missionaries tell of their work in far flung areas of the world like South East Asia or Africa, and they talk about witchcraft and occult religions, it is very easy to understand the reality of conflict. But here in our sophisticated silicon-chip society it is easy to forget the reality of the spiritual conflict in which we are engaged. We forget it at our peril.

Although most of us are willing to admit that there probably is some form of spiritual battle, in the main the church has only given lip service to this truth. Some pray regularly for 'the church militant here on earth' but it is painfully obvious that the church has become as small a fighting force as 'Dad's Army'. We fail to take seriously the reality of the enemy and we fail to see the potential of our authority. The number of churches that teach and talk specifically about the reality of spiritual battle is very small indeed.

But I say it again. God today is raising up an army. In Ezekiel's vision of the dry bones, there was a clear end result in the purposes of God. First of course, it was to reveal the glory and the power of God in renewing his people. But secondly it was in the restoration of an army, a great host of men who would fight in the Lord's battle. As the Lord is restoring his church today, it must be to produce an army to march and trample his enemies under foot.

Some of us sing with great enthusiasm the chorus *Our God Reigns* which is a cry of encouragement to one another that God is on the throne. But it is also true to say that the church reigns. As we are in Christ and Christ is seated in authority over his enemies, so it is true that we are in a position of rulership with him. Our failure to express this rulership may well be reflected in the apparent chaos of our society. We are called to be a fighting people.

This chapter is not designed to give a detailed study in spiritual warfare, but to underline again the supreme importance for the people of God to grasp this vital principle. We are not intended to wait until the church is restored before we begin to fight. The battle is on now. It is at the very gates. When Paul wrote to the Ephesians a letter outlining the pattern of New Testament church life, right at the end he underlined and emphasized the aspect of warfare. We must take this emphasis to heart.

Dangers

There are certain dangers in touching on this subject in a brief manner because there are so many common misunderstandings. Some will completely dismiss this sort of teaching out of hand. Others will see it and be excited by it, but the enemy will snatch this seed of truth out of their lives and it will soon be forgotten. Others will fall into the trap of seeing everything as either of divine origin or of the devil. They see everything that is not of God to be of the evil one, and so give him far more credit than he deserves! There are vast areas of difficulty in life which are due to purely natural or human factors, normal weakness, expressions of the flesh, physical sickness, which can so often be seen as demonic activity when in fact they are not. Plain old-fashioned sin is at the heart of most of our problems, and we must not in any way lessen human responsibility.

Many of our difficulties take time to work out and to be worked through. Sometimes we see the devil as the source of our problem because we want an easy solution. There has, too, been an unhealthy increase in what is called 'the deliverance ministry' despite no such ministry being found in the New Testament. Midwives are the only people who can exercise such a ministry! We are called to cast out evil spirits, but only as and when they present themselves to us.

However, at the risk of being 'unbalanced to create a balance' I wish now to stress the reality and the immediacy of the battle in which we are engaged.

Let us be absolutely clear that the enemy we are dealing with and talking about is personal, intelligent, organized, powerful and evil. His name is Satan, or the devil, and he is accompanied by a vast array of evil spirits. His conflict is with God and he is at work in the world to destroy all that God has made and all that he is doing. If we are to stand with Christ, then we are associated with him in the battle against his enemies. All of us in the church are engaged in this battle whether we like it or not, and we are called to fight.

There are four key ways in which we will be engaged in conflict.

1. The personal fight

This is not the place for a full discussion of the enemy's strategy against a Christian's individual walk with the Lord. But it does have some bearing on the restoration of God's church, and we must consider that here.

Probably Satan's greatest work towards the individual is in deception. Any person who is really seeking the will of God and longs to be led by the Spirit is also very vulnerable to deception. Many are being led aside by wild and wonderful schemes that are full of their own imaginings. So although they may be very active in apparently spiritual things, they are in fact busy in the devil's work because they have been sidetracked by him. Because these thoughts and desires are apparently spiritual ones we are very easily deceived. That is why we need the protection and the advice of other people. If you do not believe you are vulnerable to deception, then you are already deceived.

Another favourite attack of the enemy is to feed us with negative thoughts about others. We seem almost to delight in the criticism of others in the church, whereas instead we should be developing an attitude of love and mutual respect.

Half the secret of winning the battle is to understand that you are in it. And in all of this the Lord's words ring out to us: 'Fear not.' Paul says, 'Be strong in the Lord'—we are called to walk in victory with Christ. We need each other, so that we can be protected from deception and a negative attitude.

2. The battle for the family

As the family is so strategic in God's purposes, so it is a prime area for attack. The enemy is a divider and his work is to set husbands and wives against each other and children against their parents. Do not presume that it will come necessarily through arguments and furious rows, although it may. The enemy is often far more cunning than that. Look at the ways in which your family is being divided and see how easy it is for you to drift apart.

This is particularly true of those who are involved in much Christian work. They find their lives are so busy with Christian things and church activities, or they are dashing around the country madly to meetings, that their home is being neglected. Satan is not going to knock at the door and announce 'I'm the devil, I've come to destroy your family life; may I come in?' He doesn't wait for your invitation to arrive, but be sure of this, he will have to pack his bags and leave when he is told to go.

The first priority of every Christian, after his walk with the Lord, is his family, over and above all his church activities. The call to restore God's church must not mean the neglect of family life.

Husbands, fight for your families! Parents, fight for your children! When attacks started during the rebuilding programme of the wall of Jerusalem, Nehemiah took the following action:

In the lowest parts of the space behind the wall, in open places, I stationed the people according to their families, with their swords, their spears, and their bows. And I looked, and arose, and said to the nobles and to the officials and to the rest of the people, 'Do not be afraid of them. Remember the Lord, who is great and terrible, and fight for your brethren, your sons, your daughters, your wives, and your homes.' [Neh 4:13-14.]

3. The local church

Have you noticed how often renewal seems to go so far in a place and then stop? A lot of individuals get blessed, but it falls short of there being any real change in the life of the local body. We blame certain people, and see them as the prime reason why nothing is really happening.

Although there is nearly always personal and corporate sin involved, behind it all we need to see that there is a power at work which can only tolerate renewal as long as it remains a matter of personal enjoyment and individual blessing. The enemy will not tolerate a body of people who start to get serious, forgive one another, strive for reconciliation, and take a fresh look at church structures in the light of God's leading. If this group then takes seriously their responsibility for reaching the world outside, things have really got serious and the enemy will not take it sitting down. If you want to see the local church built, you have to fight all the way. But warfare is positive. It draws people together and encourages them in a sense of victory.

Look again at Nehemiah:

> When Sanballat and Tobiah and the Arabs and the Ammonites and the Ashdodites heard that the repairing of the walls of Jerusalem was going forward and that the breaches were beginning to be closed, they were very angry; and they all plotted together to come and fight against Jerusalem *and to cause confusion in it*. And we set up a committee to try and sort out the mess, but nobody could agree what should be done so we put off a decision for six months while we all decided to go away and think about the problem. . . .

Sorry, that should read:

> And we prayed to our God, and set a guard as a protection against them day and night. [Neh 4:7–9.]

When Paul wrote his famous exhortation to stand and fight, in Ephesians 6, he wrote it not for Christians in isolation but for the church. It was a call collectively to put on the armour of God and to stand against the forces of darkness and to pray. When Jesus talked about building his church he said that the gates of hell should not prevail against it. He associated the building of his church with conflict—and with victory.

Are there any major hindrances to the work of God in your area? Do you pray or do you complain? Have you set up a guard or have you set up a committee? You must set up a prayer guard if you are going to see the work of God develop.

Key to victory

The key to victory in these areas is righteousness. The only way that we individually can walk in victory day by day is as we keep ourselves from sin. The only way we'll experience this victory in our homes is if we have got God's pattern for the family and order in relationships right. Otherwise we'll be fighting a losing battle.

The key to seeing victory in the church is getting priorities, relationships, structures, etc, in line with biblical revelation and founded on scriptural principles.

The armour of God with which we will stand against the evil one has primarily to do with righteousness.

4. The world

The Bible tells us that 'the earth is the Lord's and the fullness thereof, the world and those who dwell therein' (Ps 24:1), although at the same time it talks about Satan as the prince of this world. If the world and those who dwell in it are by right the Lord's, then evangelism is winning them back from the hand of the enemy. In Colossians 1:13 we read, 'He has delivered us from the dominion of darkness and transferred us to the kingdom of his beloved Son.'

Evangelism is bound to involve warfare. It is not merely intellectually convincing somebody of truth, nor is it emotionally moving them by passionate appeals. It is releasing them from the lies, the deceit and the blindness of the enemy, and bringing them into the family of God. If we are to win men and women for Christ, we must engage in spiritual battle in an aggressive way and attack the strongholds of evil. Our major weapons for this task are *prayer*, *praise*, *preaching*, and *protest*.

(a) Prayer

Primary evidence that revival is among us will be an upsurge of prayer in the nation, and it is encouraging to see that in certain places this is beginning to happen. If there is to be an outpouring of the Spirit, this pattern of 'unusual' prayer will be seen everywhere. It was interesting that, during the riots of July 1981, in many cities Christians of all backgrounds and ages got together to pray, and they saw very specific answers to their prayers. But how quickly the prayer meetings stopped when the riots stopped—and the source of the problem was not dealt with. Does God have to bring riots and revolution to bring the church to pray? Is that the only way that we will take the situation seriously?

Every day we see the atrocities in Northern Ireland, but it moves us enough only to make a comment. Most of us are blind to real spiritual forces behind Northern Ireland's problems, and to the fact that there is a direct link with the riots of Britain. When people are throwing stones in the shops at the end of your street then you begin to pray! In the Old Testament we find that God responded to his people when they cried to him, and 'cry' is a strong emotional word. It is the response of desperate people.

I have been to charismatic churches that say they no longer need intercession, they just worship the Lord! If we understand the workings of God at all, and we see the evidence of history, then we know that God is a God who is moved by prayer. It is really as simple and as profound as that. You ask why the church in Korea has grown so fast. Then don't look for the answer merely in technique and methods, or wonderful pastors, but look at the thousands gathered to pray every day with deep cries from the heart. Wherever you see great growth in the church, you will see people who pray. God is dealing with us in Britain according to our prayers. We have what we pray for. Hence the mess!

It is not just a call to attend prayer meetings, but a call to extraordinary prayer—that is, times of special prayer, even at night or early in the morning before the day has begun. When will we learn that God achieves in a short space of time through the prayers of his people what it takes us years to achieve by discussion, perspiration and vast sums of money? We find it incredibly hard to get down to prayer. Could it be that it is the greatest threat to Satan and that therefore his greatest concern is to prevent it? We need to pray:

To hear from God

We cannot work alone in the spiritual battle, or we fight blind. We must see the battle and the layout of the troops, the centres of activity. The Lord is the commander and it is his battle. All he requires of us is obedience. How can we obey if we do not hear? How can we hear if we do not pray?

I remember being involved in organizing two Christian events. On the one we had spent half the committee meeting in prayer which at first made a lot of us frustrated. But the business we achieved in the rest of the time, and the decisions made, seemed to be so easy and quick. In the other we had 'opened with prayer' (after all it was a Christian gathering!) and the business always seemed to struggle and often ended with a lot of frustration. Jesus is head of the church—why don't we let him speak to us?

When Joshua crossed Jordan as the newly appointed leader of Israel, he met a man with a sword in his hand (Joshua 5: 13–15). His question was typical of our comments to the Lord: 'Are you for us, or for our adversaries?' Again and again we organize an event and then muster prayer support to get God behind it. The man replied to Joshua, 'No; but as commander of the army of the Lord I have now come.' In other words, 'I am the Lord and I am in charge!' Joshua's response was to worship him. Then he received instructions as to how to take Jericho, which were certainly not the ones Joshua had in mind! They were not in the 'Manual for successful generalship'. If God commands something, he blesses it. If he doesn't command it, his blessing is purely out of his love for his children and the event itself is never very fruitful.

The Lord will not reveal the 'deep things' of warfare and the specific details of demonic activity to those who would treat it lightly. Those who determine to press through over a period of committed intercession will receive those clear directions which are the key to victory.

To ask

When we have heard from God we need to ask for what he has told us to ask for. Those sorts of prayers have an amazing success rate and are very faith-building! When God gives his 'Amen' (it is so) and we can confidently cry 'Amen' (let it be so) then that which we ask for is assured.

To ask for the Spirit

Prayer is a demonstration of dependence. When we try to win people for Christ and fail, when we have planned great events with famous speakers and we are honest enough to realize that we have not achieved much, we begin to get desperate. Desperate people pray. The Lord gives water to the thirsty. Those that want their own glory merely work hard. Those who want God to have the glory also pray hard. The need today is not for bigger and better evangelists but for a greater outpouring of the Spirit. He came at Pentecost at a prayer meeting. He has come in times of revival through unusual prayer. He will come in power again as people pray and express their longing for him.

To fight

It is in the place of prayer that the battle for the hearts of men and women is won and the direction of nations is decided. Churches are built through prayer and individuals are rescued and restored through prayer. We need to rediscover the type of prayer that not only asks but also declares. Rulers when exercising authority do not beg or beseech, they command. We often feel it is presumptuous to pray in this way and so we ask the Lord to do it. We are told to submit ourselves to God and resist the devil. But resisting means addressing him head on and issuing a word of command.

We do have to be careful to avoid fly-swatting at the devil. If we are to be effective we must have God's directions and not just start 'binding the devil' at will. Until you know exactly where and when God wants you to stand against evil, you will be batting the air with your prayers. But as we learn to listen to the Lord and desire to stand against the enemy, so God will direct us how to resist and pull down every stronghold.

(b) Praise

This is our second weapon in the battle for the souls of men and women.

> Praise the Lord! Let the high praises of God be in their throats and two-edged swords in their hands, to wreak vengeance on the nations and chastisement on the peoples, to bind their kings with chains and their nobles with fetters of iron, to execute on them the judgment written! This is glory for all his faithful ones. Praise the Lord. [Psalm 149:1, 6–9.]

What an amazing statement: 'this is glory for all his faithful ones.' What is? Seeing the enemies of God destroyed. But what is equally amazing is the means by which this can be accomplished—praise. Why is God teaching his people to praise him? Why was the Wesleyan revival accompanied by an outpouring of hymns of praise? Because it is in praise that the victory of the Lord is declared. God doesn't teach us to praise for our own benefit, to give us a thrill, but to make a proclamation that he rules. Here we see God's highest purpose in giving us the gift of music. In the Old Testament, the musicians were there first and foremost to praise God and lead the people in praise.

One secret of victory over the powers of darkness for the life of the church and for reaching the world is for believers to express strong praise. It's good to see that not only organs and guitars are being used in praise. Those with gifts to play all sorts of musical instruments are allowing God to use them for his praise. Whole orchestras can be used, with dynamic and uplifting results.

Praise will always be something that the enemy attempts to prevent. I suppose that's why the music in a church is so important and often an area of great problem. It is essential that the person in charge of music in a church has a heart to praise the Lord first, and musical ability second. The tragedy is that the Lord can be used to worship music instead of music being used to worship the Lord. The church that has its music released to praise God is one that will experience victories day by day. The devil hates praise. It scatters his forces in panic.

(c) Preaching

Preaching is the declaration of truth. It should challenge the mind, for the gospel makes its appeal at the rational level. If a man is to be converted he is to be convinced. It should challenge the conscience and the emotions, for the gospel challenges the moral standing of a man and speaks to him of the holiness and love of God.

But preaching also breaks the hold of evil over the individual. It declares truth, and truth liberates. Primarily it speaks of the cross. The power of preaching the cross comes not in its intellectual compulsion but in its ability to convict of sin and to proclaim the victory over the powers of evil. Hence it allows a man to respond to the call of love. Preaching in the context of prayer and praise is at its most powerful. So much of our evangelism tends to border on entertainment and a desire not to offend at all costs, but preaching is often offensive—although the preacher as a person should never be.

It is very interesting to see music and drama in the context of preaching. Each on its own could easily become entertainment and preaching on its own can be lifeless and cerebral. In the past the great preachers painted pictures with words. Today the same thing is happening, except that the pictures are now expressed through drama and sometimes through music. Where it is illustrative to preaching, drama is at its most effective. Proclamation in praise or preaching will always be effective if done with the love and compassion of Jesus towards the people, and with aggression and purpose towards the devil.

(d) Protest

'People in Britain won't hate you if you stand for Jesus, but they will if you stand for righteousness.' So said a friend recently. In 1971 the impact made by the Festival of Light in the country, the ripples of which were felt for many years afterwards, caused the reaction it did because it stood against evil in a particular form. It is often quoted that 'evil triumphs when good men do nothing'. The church of Jesus Christ must speak out against injustice, corruption and unrighteousness, whether it be local or national, whether it be individuals, governments or large companies. We are not called to be pious or holier than thou, but we are called to be a prophetic voice standing against evil in the world.

Soldiers for Christ

The call to battle is not a call to cheap triumphalism, it is to blood, sweat and tears! It is a call to lay down our lives under the lordship of Christ. It will be a long hard fight. Paul wrote to Timothy: 'Take your share of suffering as a good soldier of Christ Jesus. No soldier on service gets entangled in civilian pursuits, since his aim is to satisfy the one who enlisted him' (2 Tim 2: 3–4). We read in the book of Revelation: 'They have conquered him [Satan] by the blood of the Lamb and by the word of their testimony, for they *loved not their lives even unto death.'* The promised land was not taken in a day, it was taken little by little. It involved fighting and hardship, but it was on the basis of assured victory that they pressed forward.

God's call-up today is not for a banner-waving rally but for a life of service and conflict in his army. But victory is sure as we take the land.

11

Evangelism and the body

The reasons for the lack of effective evangelism in Britain over the past years are numerous, and it would be wrong to say that there was one particular reason above all the others. But I think certain observations are valid.

The overriding factor is that there is a sense in which God has withheld this blessing so that the church is equipped for harvesting. Although this is a divine work there is also human responsibility.

Evangelist or witness

Every believer is a witness for Christ. He may be an effective or an ineffective one, but he is a witness. Not everyone is an evangelist. But the failure of growth is not in the main due to the failure of evangelists, although we have been painfully slow in recognizing those with that gift in the church, and also guilty of allowing those who are active to remain isolated from church life. No; it is the failure of ordinary people to share their faith. There is no doubt that the church, as a human body, grows faster through multiplication (everyone wins one) than by addition (mass evangelism). Ultimately, the only way we are going to have a significant effect on this country is not primarily through mass evangelism but through *mass witness*.

If Billy Graham came to Britain and preached every single night in a different place, and every night a thousand people were converted, how long would it take him to reach the whole nation for Christ? Actually it would take more than 135 years. If every believer brought somebody else to Christ just once a year, and those people in their turn brought somebody else to Christ once a year, how long would it take us to reach every person for Christ in this nation? *It would take only seven years!* Now I know that's only theoretical and playing with statistics, and ignores a lot of other factors—some have far greater ability to share their faith than others—but it's helpful to see that the fastest way to reach people for Christ is through personal witness. Do you see the tremendous speed with which Britain could be won for Christ if each one of us were filled with the Holy Spirit and enabled and willing to witness for him? We need mass evangelism because we need to evangelize the masses! But preaching and mass evangelism, although important, only work well in the environment of personal witness.

What a tragedy it would be to see thousands of people coming to Christ only to see them lost again because there was no structure into which they could be fitted, where they could be helped, strengthened and encouraged.

Why is it not happening?

One outstanding reason is that most of us attempt evangelism at arm's length. Let me quote from Derek Cook of Maranatha Ministries:

> Evangelism is on every church's agenda, mentioned at all the conferences and talked about in all the best circles. But evangelism does not seem to be the *priority* for anyone at all! If all the Christians who attend this year's conventions were laid end to end, how far would they stretch? Would they reach as far as their next door neighbours or their colleagues? We are not desperate about evangelism. Evangelism is far too costly for us in terms of money, time and love. We are just playing at evangelism. Mere play-actors. Hypocrites is the New Testament Greek word that describes us perfectly!

Strong words maybe, but they need to be said, and need to be heard and responded to.

But when we grasp the reality of the church in the locality, the home group in our street, we begin to get a vision and a burden for our neighbours. Where people meet together they can pray for specific people until they see them come into the kingdom. When you live near people you get to know their needs and can relate Christ to them. People at last can begin to see the love of Christ in action. When we really get to grips with the reality of the local body of Christ, it will revolutionize our evangelism. It will not only mean that we have a concern for the people who live right next to us, but it will mean that we have an understanding of the different gifts that it takes not only to bring people to Christ, but to help them grow in Christ. It means that between us we can effectively reach our neighbourhood and make disciples for Jesus.

The key

The key to evangelism in the future lies in the home. God is at work in the streets and houses of our country—so it is there that we too must work.

Two Christian families live near us in a cul-de-sac with twenty-six houses in it. They decided recently to invite the entire road to one of the houses so that people could get to know each other. They also told the people in the letter of invitation they sent round that they wanted to share their faith in Jesus Christ. Now, I thought that would immediately drive people away! But these couples already knew, at least by name, everyone in the road, and had some sort of relationship with them. The amazing thing was that practically every house was represented at the gathering, which included some food and coffee and a short bit of testimony. The sense of appreciation was tremendous. Even those who claimed to be atheists went away saying how much they had been interested by what was said and done. But their interest was founded on the care and concern shown by their hosts for them as people and not just souls to be saved. It takes tremendous courage to do that, but the rewards are enormous. What if everybody began praying and reaching out to their neighbours in that way? This sort of thing is happening in a lot of different places, but at the moment it is being done by isolated individuals who have a vision for it. There is no limit to what can be done in the home if only we have the faith and courage. What about street parties organized by Christians?

But what if these people do come to Christ? If you already have home groups going, how natural to feed them into that, rather than just sending them to the nearest establishment to sit in a pew for an hour on Sunday.

It's so exciting to see, too, how many women are using the tremendous opportunities that arise during the day. Women's Bible study and prayer groups are springing up, meeting every week and with a monthly guest coffee morning. Many people are coming to Christ through this very natural and practical means. It certainly beats being a working mum rushing out to earn a bit more money to pay for the second car that you must have if you are going out to work! What an impact women with vision and love can have on a locality.

Then there are the men, of course. Let the men reach the men! It would be foolish to ignore the reality that for a woman, her sphere of contact is the home and the vicinity in which she lives, whereas for the man with a job, he has other areas of contact with people as well. Therefore, it is only right and natural that he should use the environment God has put him in, in order to share his faith. His business, and the social life that results from it for him and his wife, will open up opportunities to witness for Christ. The Full Gospel Businessmen's Fellowship International is an example of an organization that has been set up to encourage these areas of contact and opportunity.

It sounds easy on paper, but of course it is not, because it costs a great deal to make the effort to reach out and then be prepared for the people to know where you stand. It is acceptable to be a church-goer today, but not a person who loves and trusts Jesus and is willing to let others know about it.

Street-level

The growth of what can best be described as 'Christian alternatives to the pub', that is coffee shops, restaurants, etc—is rapid all across the country. They are the direct result of this desire to reach the man in the street actually in the street. They represent an attempt to bring the church down to street-level.

Jesus said go into all the world. We have continually said to the world, 'Come into the church.' At last we are beginning to take the gospel to the streets. There is no reason why coffee-shops, restaurants and so forth should not spring up everywhere as an expression of united church life in each locality. There are always plenty of people willing to provide manpower which enables the costs to be kept down. People usually say money is the problem. But there is plenty of money around, it's just that it has got stuck in people's pockets! It's only a matter or priority, as we usually have money for what we really want.

The church too is rich with resources in terms of manpower and ability. Electricians, builders and the like are there if we look around. Many of them are ready and willing to be involved. Most people hold back not through lack of vision, but because the task appears too big. What happened to faith? 'Great is the Lord' and 'Our God Reigns' we sing on Sunday, but where is that God on Monday? We would be amazed at what was achieved if more people stepped out in faith.

Faith is always dependent on first hearing God's word for that situation. There are plenty who start out in faith, continue in hope and end up in charity! In those cases faith is replaced by presumption. But if God gives us a word to go forward, we must express faith through obedience.

God is wanting to do so much more than we give him scope for. Have you ever thought of a hairdressing salon run by Christians? Where else do you have people captive and relaxed and wanting to chat for such a long period of time? And they cannot easily run out in the middle! One Christian I know owned the only bakery on a housing estate. Soon he came to know everybody on the estate because they all came to him for bread.

Christian doctors have tremendous opportunities. Unfortunately too many are concerned with getting to the top, and look on G.P. work as second-rate. If you want to meet all the people in need in the area, come and be a G.P. (Get qualified first!) It's nonsense to say that it's bad etiquette to share Christ in a surgery! It's usually just fear. The possibilities are endless, or as far as our faith will take us. We cannot be used beyond that, but it is amazing how faith grows if we see it rewarded at first in small ways.

For too long we as Christians have opted out because the welfare state appeared to offer so much, but more and more we are seeing its inadequacies. The things that we have taken for granted and allowed the state to provide for people are soon going to have to be provided once again by the church. The whole issue of Christian schools is again being discussed, and in certain places in Britain, new schools are being started by Christians. It is early days and much careful thought is still needed. Although this is still much in discussion, because of the decline in education standards in Britain it cannot be very long before Christians are forming many such schools.

'But,' you say, 'it's all very well you talking like that if you live in the south of England. After all the keen people all seem to sink to the bottom of the country, and in the northern towns there are vast areas with no Christians at all.' Althought that is certainly true, I wonder how many more people have been called to work in the north than have responded to God's call to go. Also it is time the strong churches began to send people out into the more difficult areas to found new churches. In many places there is a surplus of manpower and resources. Where the resources outweigh the need in any given locality, then people should be made up into teams and sent elsewhere. The strong churches could send people, money and resources into big housing areas to found new churches; maybe groups of people should even move out of one locality into another, with a church-founding motivation. But once these are set up, strong churches must not dominate, but let the new churches have their independence. They simply need to be available to help where necessary.

There must be apostolic gifts in the church today. Each local church may well have a church-planting capacity within it. But if we are expecting to see apostolic gifts in the local church, we obviously shouldn't expect to see them working in the locality from which they come, because there is already a church there!

The evangelism sieve

If thousands of people came to Christ today, then a large number would flounder. There is not enough to hold them. That does not deny the power of the Holy Spirit, but it does recognize the need for the right pattern in which growth can take place. If the church is not ready to cope, we will have a tragedy on our hands. We might have a revival that lasts a few years, but it would soon wane again. If we have renewal and revival without restoration of the local church, we will not see a lasting change in the country. But if the local body has found itself, and has a structure of cell division, then there is no limit to the number of people that it can cope with and discipline and enable to grow. Now is the time to build for growth, not by extending the building, but by building the body. We need to unite in order to be able to continually divide! We don't need more church buildings—we already have vast numbers of houses, and public buildings are numerous.

The body and unemployment

I suppose the greatest social issue at the present time is that of high unemployment. How long will it be before there are five million people out of work?—and the number is still rising. Some of those people have never had a job. Others have reached an age where they will probably never have full employment again, and others are in the prime of their lives and have had their secure jobs taken from under them. What a problem, with vast numbers of disillusioned, bored and comparatively poor people around. But also what an opportunity! We are still in the shock situation where the problem has arisen but no long-term planning has been done to cope with it, partly because few people will publicly admit that it is a long-term issue. We have an immediate and a long-term responsibility, in both of which Christians can take the initiative and be in the forefront.

The short-term situation

It is vitally important for the unemployed Christian to understand how the Lord feels about his situation and that God has it completely under control. He is very easily filled with a sense of rejection. A friend of mine referred to it as being similar to having a bereavement. Nobody will really talk about it, or if they do it's only with embarrassment. But the Lord has a message to the unemployed Christian. It is this: 'The Lord has need of you.' You thought you were being made redundant but the Lord 'released you from where you were tied' (Mk 11).

In the short-term there are two basic things that the unemployed person needs. The first is money. For many supplementary benefit enables them to survive, but not much more. The second is work. Work brings along with it dignity, status, self-confidence and well-being. We have always in the past defined work as employed work. The Bible says if a man will not work he shall not eat. But what is work? Surely helping in the community is work. Providing for those in need is work. Evangelism is work. Prayer is work. We have to completely rethink the whole concept of what work is.

Now surely it is the responsibility of the local church to provide for both of these needs. It is very easy for us to assume that the social services will provide for the needs of the unemployed. But the social services are part of the world system that is at its heart corrupt. Unemployed people go to the social security expecting to be understood and appreciated, and yet so often find that in fact they are treated just as a number, and in a very patronizing sort of way. It's because they are dealing with an impersonal system.

The danger is that the church will treat the unemployed in exactly the same way. That is, they become totally patronizing to them. First they assume that they must be all right because they are receiving dole money. Secondly they assume that because they have just about got enough to live on they don't need any more. Thirdly they very easily see them as a little bit of a nuisance. These attitudes aren't usually consciously expressed, but they are nevertheless expressed in such a way that many unemployed people feel that attitude coming across.

Furthermore, these people are one of the gifts of the Lord to the community. The amount of work both social and evangelistic that there is to do in any area is vast, and most people are crying out for manpower. It is the responsibility of the employed in any area to provide for the unemployed. But how can this be if the church is not really fellowshipping?

The long-term situation

The church today needs to be prophetic, providing and protecting.

PROPHETIC

Millions are crying out against the scandal of the unemployment situation. Yet many of these are in full-time employment and working overtime. Vast numbers of households have two wage-earners in the same home. Many of these facts in themselves demonstrate the problem. Who is going to forgo overtime? Who will give up their job for the benefit of someone else? What companies will start principles of work-sharing? The church needs to be both exposing injustice and taking a lead in developing new patterns for the future.

In the long term, although the politicians still talk in terms of returning to full employment, those who are able to be more objective see that as totally unrealistic. We are in the middle of an employment revolution associated with a revolution in technology. The whole concept of work, employment, voluntary work, leisure and so on that we have taken for granted, is changing. The old pattern of a man working forty-eight hours a week, for forty-eight weeks in the year, for forty-eight years of his life, is past! Whole new patterns of living are going to have to be worked out so that we can cope with the future of shorter employment hours and more time spent in the community.

The gap between employed and unemployed must be removed. There are vast areas where initiative must be taken and it must be taken by Christians, so that the new lifestyle patterns are based on God's value of man and where love motivates rather than greed. For this to happen, Christians have got to disentangle themselves from the rat race where people desperately try to survive and maintain their own materialistic lifestyle. Many Christians with once-secure and good jobs are being made redundant. This may be one of God's ways of shaking people into understanding the true nature of the situation that we are in.

Providing

We need in our communities to see the unemployed Christians as providing tremendous opportunity instead of great problems. Unemployment has meant that a large number of non-Christians are beginning to think seriously about life. When a man has everything he needs, he doesn't ask questions. When you take away his life supports he looks around for help. Thousands more every day are looking around for help.

The same people also have the other great evangelistic asset; time to think. A man in a hurry doesn't stop to think very deeply. Those without a job have time to think, to read, to share. If only we could put those with time to talk alongside those with time to listen! First of all we need to train and equip the unemployed and then give them a vision of what they can do. The coffee shops mentioned before are one of the bases for the unemployed to function from. As well as evangelism, there are all sorts of other ways that people can be employed. It only takes a little imagination.

Protecting

A man or woman who is unemployed needs tremendous support and protection. It is a protection from loneliness, guilt and depression. They are very vulnerable. We all find our jobs give us value and status in the world, and so to be without a job suddenly makes a person very insecure. The kind of support and care that is needed can only be given by people who live nearby and who take a personal interest in these people's lives.

Deacons

It is time to see the work of deacons in a fresh light. We need men and women like Stephen who will serve the community through helping the widows, the old, the unemployed and others in need, and not just care for the church roof.

Combine harvesting

Jesus said, 'The harvest is plentiful, but the labourers are few;

pray therefore the Lord of the harvest to thrust out labourers into his harvest field' (Lk 10:2*).

The indications are from many places and people that the tide of faith, openness and hunger in the world has turned. There isn't exactly an avalanche of people clamouring to be saved, but the tide is coming in again. If this is true, it means in the next few years we are going to see opportunities for sharing Christ increase at every level of society and in every part of the country. If the faith of the nation is turning back to God, will the church be there to lead it? I am also in no doubt that this will be accompanied by far greater hardship and persecution. The sides will become clearer.

That takes us back to the great heart cry of Jesus as he looked at the fields ready for harvest. Where are the labourers? Until recently the harvesting has been done by a few men wielding sickles desperately trying to bring in what they can. A few evangelists have worked hard and long and seen some brought into the kingdom, but in terms of overall impact it is so very little.

The urgency of the hour and the size of the task call for a combine harvester. We may need large-scale evangelism and big meetings, but they are only an aid to the really effective work. The harvester that Britain requires is that made up of hundreds of thousands of ordinary people acting as living witnesses to Christ where they are. Larger-scale evangelistic activity directed into that type of situation would then have tremendous signifi-cance and value, in order to crystallize the issues in people's minds, challenge them to commitment and envision them to go out into their world. But the key issue is the mass mobilization of men and women.

If we begin to grasp what Jesus was saying and feeling, then we must respond in the way he asked. Make it a matter of first importance to pray every day, 'Lord thrust out labourers into this area in which I live. Make every believer a labourer. Thrust them out. Encourage them. Envision them. Fill them. Use them.'

The key to evangelism in Britain is in the home. It is through the witness of Christian families where they live, sharing their faith in simple and often practical ways with those around them. The key is not what happens in a certain building on Sundays, however important that might be, but in the reality of the kingdom of God in the lives of ordinary people during the week.

The words of a song entitled *One Shall Tell Another* by Graham Kendrick summarize many of these thoughts.

> One shall tell another
> And he shall tell his friend,
> Husbands and wives and children
> Shall come following on.
> From house to house in families
> Shall more be gathered in,
> And lights will shine in every street
> So warm and welcoming.
>
> Compassion of the Father
> Is ready now to flow,
> Through acts of love and mercy
> We must let it show.
> He turns now from his anger
> To show a smiling face,
> And longs that men should stand beneath
> The fountain of his grace.
>
> He longs to do much more than
> Our faith has yet allowed,
> To thrill us and surprise us
> With his sovereign power.
> Where darkness has been darkest
> The brightest light will shine,
> His invitation comes to us,
> It's yours and it is mine.
>
> Come on in and taste the new wine,
> The wine of the kingdom,
> The wine of the kingdom of God.
> Here is healing
> And forgiveness,
> The wine of the kingdom,
> The wine of the kingdom of God.

(From *The King Is Among Us*, Kingsway Music 1982.)

12

I have a dream

Everybody is allowed to indulge in dreaming and it's very important that we do so. Dreams (I don't mean those we have when asleep) express our longings, hopes and yearnings. Sometimes they are no more than fantasy allowing us to escape from the hardship of reality. But many times God puts a dream in your heart which inspires faith, releases prayer that is more than mere words, lifts you out of complacency and takes you forward in your Christian walk. This sort of dream constitutes a goal, a vision, a place towards which you know you are heading.

The dream that many people have is for the millions in this country who have rejected Christianity, often because of the image the church has portrayed, to have the chance to see and respond to the living Christ. Twice in the New Testament we are told that 'no man has ever seen God'. In the one instance it tells us that Jesus has made him known, and in the other that we by our love can make him known. What a tremendous challenge!

I have a dream that in every street in Britain there will be a cell of people who love and care for each other and reach out in loving concern for those around them. These will be the means of sharing the love of God with the immediate neighbourhood.

I have a dream that in every local community there will be a gathering together of the cell groups to experience fellowship, worship and teaching together. In every place there will be what best can be described as a community church. These would not be in dull uniformity, copies of each other, but every one will be distinctive to its own community. They may be the remnant of denominational churches, or a new church where none existed before, or a fellowship of believers alongside the old structures. The purpose of these will be to reach out in service to those around, not merely concerned for their own needs. It will be Christ's instrument for showing his love and power to the community. New believers will be welcomed, supported, taught, encouraged, and sent out as witnesses to those around them. The worship of these churches will not consist merely of repetitive choruses and hand clapping (valid though these are) but draw on all the wealth of church liturgy past and present, so that there is a glorious variety in worship and ministry.

I have a dream that in every city there will be regular 'feast days' when these local expressions of the body of Christ meet to celebrate the Lord together and demonstrate the power of Christ in their midst. Across a city there will be sharing in gifts and ministry, where nobody is possessive of a particular work but all is done for the building up and encouraging of each other. This will truly be a serving church.

I have a dream that across every city leaders of local churches will come together often and regularly, submitting themselves to one another, forgetting their own individual needs, fighting for the city and praying for the power of God to fall.

I have a dream that God will once again have a dwelling place among men, through whose corporate life he can reveal his glory to the world.

I have a dream that God in his abundant mercy will withhold his hand of final judgement on this nation and respond to the tears of his people and come down in a great visitation among us. In this he will reach out his hand of love to millions of spiritually starving people, adding to his church in such numbers that we are in no doubt that God has been among us, working great acts of power.

Awake, awake, put on your strength, O Zion;
Put on your beautiful garments,
   O Jerusalem, the holy city;
For there shall no more come into you
   the uncircumcised and the unclean.
Shake yourself from the dust, arise,
   O captive Jerusalem;
Loose the bonds from your neck,
   O captive daughter of Zion. [Is 52:1–2.]

Also in paperback from Kingsway . . .

The Spirit of Renewal

by Edward England

What has the charismatic movement done for the church?

This is a unique survey of the events and controversies surrounding this exciting move of God's Spirit from the early sixties through to the eighties. Here are the stories of renewed Christians and renewed churches.

Based on the first 100 issues of *Renewal* magazine this is a vivid portrayal of the blessings and the tensions—dealing with such vital issues as prophecy, praise, tongues, evangelism, social action, Christian unity, and conflict with the 'establishment'.

Edward England, formerly Religious Publishing Director of Hodder and Stoughton, is now the publisher of *Renewal*. The editor is Michael Harper.

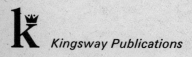

Kingsway Publications

The Radical Christian

by Arthur Wallis

God's Holy Spirit is at work to change us into the likeness of Christ. Do we realize what a radical change this means?

This book challenges us to re-examine some of our cherished customs and beliefs. It shows how Scripture can guide us over such issues as church unity, water and Spirit baptism, and denominational loyalty.

The author confesses that this has not been an easy book to write. Nor will it be easy for us to receive. It calls for a verdict on God's truth— and so for a verdict on ourselves. Each one of us must decide: am I a compromiser, or a radical?

The axe is laid to the root of the tree.

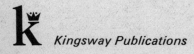

Kingsway Publications

Built to Last

by Ron Trudinger

When Ron Trudinger wrote *Cells for Life* many churches were discovering the advantages of subdividing into home groups.

Since then a sequel has become necessary, because there is a real danger of introducing home groups as little more than a church face-lift. If the principles underlying church restoration are not understood, there will be no lasting benefit for the church. 'Restoration' is the necessary return to clear biblical patterns of church structure.

In this book Ron Trudinger (a pastor at Basingstoke Community Church) draws on his experience of restoration church life to apply the Bible's teaching in a direct and practical way.

k
Kingsway Publications

Moving on in the Spirit

by Dennis Bennett

All over the world Christians have been experiencing a new love for God and a new freedom in praise and worship. Gifts of healing have been rediscovered, and churches have come alive by the renewing work of the Spirit.

This book starts from there. It encourages us to continue on the course that God has set, but also points out some of the pitfalls which lie in our path.

Dennis Bennett challenges some of the wrong ideas that are infiltrating many Christian circles today—including misunderstandings about praise, healing, and the acceptance of all things as God's will.

Knowing the truth on such important issues will enable us to 'think the thoughts of God', helping us to understand his purposes and so move on in the Spirit.

Dennis Bennett is the author of the bestseller
Nine O'Clock in the Morning,
and (with his wife Rita),
The Holy Spirit and You.

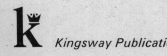

Kingsway Publications